Twentieth Century Christians

TWENTIETH CENTURY CHRISTIANS

CHRISTIANS

Twelve Mini-Biographies

JOHN D. SEARLE

THE SAINT ANDREW PRESS
EDINBURGH

First published 1977 by
THE SAINT ANDREW PRESS
121 George Street, Edinburgh

© 1977 John D. Searle

ISBN 0 7152 0367 3

Printed and bound in Great Britain by
T. & A. Constable Ltd., Edinburgh.

Contents

To

All who express their Faith in action

There is no doubt in my mind that it is the people with a religious motivation who keep the less attractive forms of voluntary social effort going. They provide a large proportion of those who are willing to offer their services and their life and who are least prepared to give in when the pressures build up. . . .'

Commander Arthur Hague, when Home Office Adviser on Voluntary Work in the After-Care of Prisoners; formerly General Secretary of the Royal National Mission to Deep Sea Fisherman

Introduction

The story of a life lived significantly is always worth hearing. Since the first century A.D. the lives of great Christians have been a source both of interest and of inspiration. They have also provided a valuable testimony to the efficacy of the Christian Faith. As such they have been, and continue to be, an important part of Christian education and advocacy. They are of particular value today when very few children, young people or adults are willing to listen to the claims of the gospel presented directly. Increasing use is made of biography—of lives that speak for themselves—not only in Church-based programmes of Christian education, but also in religious and moral education generally.*

Many young people who grew up during the first half of this century became familiar with stirring tales of such heroes of the Faith as Elizabeth Fry, David Livingstone, William Booth, Mary Slessor, Albert Schweitzer and Toyohiko Kagawa. The lives of such great men and women still merit our study, but a new generation needs, in addition, more recent examples of Christianity expressed in action.

Happily, there are many Christians born in the twentieth century whose life stories bear impressive testimony to the continuing influence of the Christian religion. Many of these have been the subject of full-length biographies. *The aim of this*

* See the Note on the use of biographies for Religious Education in School at the conclusion of this Introduction.

book is two-fold. First, to provide something in between the longer biographies written for adults and the brief, simplified 'lives' written for children. Secondly, it aims to provide up-to-date information about those whose story was first published some years ago, and to show how the work they initiated has subsequently developed.

A chapter is devoted to each life-story and the chapters are arranged in chronological order according to the subject's date of birth. The principal difficulty has been the selection of persons to include. Out of so many worthy of consideration, those that are included were chosen to represent a varied cross-section of Christians who, in different ways, have made notable contributions to the well-being of their fellow men and women.

It is hoped that this book will meet the needs of those who either do not have access to, or the time to read, the full-length biographies available. *It is intended for use by several different categories of reader:*

1. For individual reading by adolescents and adults.
2. For speakers who require a talk—or a series of talks—at church meetings, e.g. fellowship meetings, men's meetings, women's meetings and suchlike.
3. For use in church worship, abbreviated and adapted as necessary, e.g. in young people's services, parade services and family services; for use (with, or without, audio-visual aids) in a series of special services featuring the lives and work of twentieth century Christians, perhaps commemorating the anniversary of their birth or death; or for use as illustrative materials for sermons and addresses.
4. For use in Bible Classes, Youth Fellowships, and Sunday School to supplement, or as an alternative to, other teaching material; and also for use in Youth Club Epilogues.
5. For use in Religious Education (or Moral Education) in Schools—see the Note following this Introduction.

In compiling these mini-biographies, I have used a variety of sources, including direct contact with the persons concerned. In the main, however, they are based on the literature detailed in the lists of further reading, and I wish to express my thanks to the authors and publishers who have allowed me to quote from their publications. I have endeavoured to acknowledge the source of direct quotations, but if any material has been included for which permission should have been sought, I offer my apologies.

If the story is about someone still living, the chapter has been read and approved by the person concerned or by a nominated representative of the organisation with which his work is associated. This has enabled me to include up-to-date material and to make some corrections to facts presented in previous publications; I am most grateful for this help. I am indebted to Jean Holm, Principal Lecturer in Religious Studies at Homerton College, Cambridge, for allowing me to quote from a chapter on Biographies in her book *Teaching Religion in School*. I am also grateful to several others: to my father-in-law, the Revd Dr C. Leslie Mitton for reading the manuscript and offering many helpful suggestions; to Mrs Jennifer Link for typing the first draft of the manuscript; to the Publishers for their courtesy and efficiency; and also to those who listened when these life-stories were first presented in an abbreviated form in a series of monthly talks. However, my greatest debt of gratitude must be to those who are featured in the chapters that follow. It is my hope that those who read or hear these mini-biographies will find their interest stimulated to learn more, not only of the lives presented here, but also of *the* Life which inspired them all.

JOHN D. SEARLE

A NOTE ON THE USE OF BIOGRAPHIES FOR RELIGIOUS EDUCATION IN SCHOOL

It is assumed that some adaptation and abbreviation will be necessary in order to use these biographies effectively in the *Church-based* settings outlined in the Introduction (2, 3, 4).

The use of this type of biography for Religious Education in *School* poses some *particular* problems. These are outlined by Jean Holm in her book *Teaching Religion in School*, Oxford University Press, 1975. She points out that biographies can be used for two purposes. First, to demonstrate the relationship between faith and life by using examples in which 'the relationship is explicit and the beliefs are the acknowledged driving force of the person's life' (p. 34). Second, with regard to the 'implicit element in R.E.' they may be used to help pupils to 'explore and reflect upon human experience' (p. 40).

Jean Holm believes that, in the non-confessional context of school, any general use of biographies should not begin before the age of nine, and that their use to illustrate the relationship between a person's explicitly held beliefs and his life should be confined to the secondary school. She feels that, even then, they should be used very sparingly with eleven- to thirteen-year-olds. Not all educationalists will accept the need to restrict the use of biography quite so strictly. However, few will disagree that the use of biographical material is *particularly* useful with those over thirteen, because young people of this age are better equipped mentally to understand the nature of religious belief and they are also better able to compare alternative systems of belief.

Jean Holm maintains that in *School* our task is 'neither to teach for belief nor to initiate children into any one religious tradition' (p.40). Consequently, those who share this objective approach to Religious Education will need to supplement the life-stories contained in this book with biographies of those who are *not* Christian, or who do not hold *any* particular *religious* belief, but who are nonetheless clearly motivated by belief of some kind.

Another problem arises in using the stories of such Christians as Gladys Aylward and Brother Andrew, in which deliverance from crises and the supply of material needs are regarded as direct answers to prayer. Whereas adolescents are sufficiently mature to be able to discuss the particular belief in the efficacy of prayer held by Gladys Aylward and by Brother Andrew, younger children may be left with the impression of a series of dramatic 'magical' interventions by an all-powerful God. This illustrates the importance of selecting the subject and adapting the presentation of the story to the children's stage of development.

It is also necessary, as Jean Holm reminds us, to ensure that the 'background and experience of the pupils are sufficient to enable them to appreciate the qualities of the person being studied' (p. 36). For instance, the work of Martin Luther King, Jr is best understood in the milieu of racialism in the USA, and that of Mario Borrelli in relation to post-war social conditions in Naples; and if we are to avoid giving the impression that Germany is our natural enemy and that the Japanese are habitually cruel, the stories of Leonard Cheshire, John Dodd and Ernest Gordon need careful setting within their respective historical contexts.

Jean Holm also makes the point that it is better for school pupils to study a small number of biographies thoroughly rather than a larger number superficially. This is one reason why, in this book, the chapters are considerably longer than would normally be required for a single lesson in school or for a talk to a church group or meeting. Those who wish to study a biography still further will find at the end of each chapter a list of books for further reading (some may now be out of print but should be available from a local library), a note of any audio-visual aids currently available, and a note of sources from which more information can be obtained.

CHAPTER ONE

Ai Weh Deh — The Virtuous One
Gladys Aylward

Born 1902

Mrs Jeannie Lawson had spent most of her life as a missionary in China. Although seventy-three years old, she had no intention of retiring, but she did need help. She had, in fact, received a letter from a girl in England offering to come to Yangcheng to be her assistant, but that was some weeks ago and Jeannie had forgotten all about it in the meanwhile.

Then, one day, she was told that there was a stranger at the gate of the Mission compound. She hurried across the courtyard and found a small, nervous-looking young woman, who bowed politely.

'And who are you?' demanded Jeannie Lawson.

'I am Gladys Aylward who wrote to you from London,' the new arrival replied.

'Oh yes. Well, are you coming in?' From her casual tone of voice, the little white-haired missionary might have been inviting-in her next-door neighbour, instead of a young woman who had travelled alone, thousands of miles to become a missionary.

When Gladys May Aylward arrived in China, she was thirty years old. She had been born in London on 24 February 1902. As a child she had received little formal education, but she had gone regularly to Sunday School and Church. As she grew older, she became impatient with anything to do with religion; her ambition was to become an actress. This, however, was not to be; and instead, at the age of fourteen, she started work as an assistant in a Penny Bazaar. Later, she took a job at a grocer's shop, and eventually became a parlourmaid in the West End of London.

One Tuesday evening, her work finished, she went out for a walk. As she was passing a church, a group of young people standing at the door invited her to come in. Half-laughing, half-protesting, she allowed herself to be taken inside. She sat through the service, compelled to listen by the eloquence of the preacher. Afterwards, as she was hurrying away, someone at the door grasped her hand, and enquiring her name, said, 'Miss Aylward, I believe that God is wanting you.'

'No fear!' Gladys replied. 'I don't want any of that!' She scurried off, but she could not rid herself of the nagging thought that even if *she* did not want God, perhaps *he* wanted her. She decided to go and see the Reverend F. W. Pitt, the minister of the church where she had been persuaded to attend the service. He was out, but his wife spent some time talking with her. Eventually, Gladys agreed that 'if God was willing to take her on', she was willing to let him. With Mrs Pitt beside her, she knelt down and accepted Jesus Christ as her Saviour.

Gladys joined the Young Life Campaign, and in one of their magazines she read an article about the millions in China who had never heard of Christ. As time went on, she became convinced that God wanted her to go there as a missionary. She was accepted for training by the China Inland Mission, but at the end of her first probationary term she was advised to leave; it was felt that due to her limited education, she would be unable to learn the difficult Chinese language.

Gladys was very disappointed, but she was still sure that God wanted her for some special task. She went to work, first in Bristol, then in Neath, and finally she returned to London. There she found work as a housemaid. She did not forget her resolve, however, and on the third day at her new job, she laid out her few possessions and prayed,

> 'O God, here's the Bible about which I long to tell others, here's my *Daily Light* that every day will give me a new

promise, and here is 2½d. If You want me, I am going to China with these.'

From that hour, she began to save every penny she could earn in order to pay her fare to China.

When she had saved enough, she was faced with the question, where in China did God want her? It was about this time that Gladys heard of Jeannie Lawson. She had come home from China after her husband had died, but could not settle in England and, in spite of her age, she had gone out again. She needed a younger person with her at Yangcheng who would be able to carry on the work that she had begun. Gladys felt sure that this was the call she had been awaiting, and wrote to Mrs Lawson offering her services.

After some weeks, she received a favourable reply. She went home, packed a couple of suitcases, and on 15 October 1932 she set off from Liverpool Street Railway Station. Her lonely journey by rail took her through Holland, Germany and Russia. Unable to cross the Russian border, she went by sea to Japan and after a long, and often terrifying journey, she eventually set foot in China. A week later, on November 16, after an uncomfortable journey on a mule, she arrived in Yangcheng and was directed to the Mission.

Yangcheng was a beautiful town built in a valley between high, bare mountains. Jeannie Lawson introduced Gladys to its people and taught her a few sentences in Chinese. No-one could pronounce her surname, so they called her Ai-weh-deh, which sounded something like Aylward, but meant 'The Virtuous One'.

Not long after Gladys arrived, Jeannie had the idea of turning the Mission courtyard into an inn where muleteers could stay overnight. This would give them the opportunity to tell their guests about Jesus Christ. They decided on a name and hung up a sign in Chinese which read, *The Inn of Eight Happinesses*. Gladys was given the task of persuading the muleteers to stop there. Her method was to wait at the gateway until a mule train approached, then she would step forward and shout, 'We have no fleas. We have no bugs. Good, good, good. Come, come, come!' She would then grab hold of the leading mule and drag it into the courtyard with the other animals following. At night, Jeannie and Mr Lu, the Chinese cook-cum-evangelist, told Bible stories to their guests. Until Gladys had learned the language, her duty was to feed the mules and scrape them clean of mud!

In addition to the work at the 'inn', Jeannie took Gladys with her when she went to preach in the surrounding villages. Slowly, Gladys picked up the language, albeit with a distinct Cockney accent! She set herself to learn some of the Bible stories by heart, and began to take her turn in telling them to the muleteers staying overnight.

Towards the end of the first year Gladys spent in China, Jeannie Lawson fell ill and died, leaving Gladys to carry on the work assisted only by Mr Lu. With a struggle she managed to keep the inn going and to continue holding regular services at the Mission. She also visited the people in their homes, giving them what medical aid she could, and, accompanied by Mr Lu, she went to the villages and preached in the market places to anyone who would listen.

Without Jeannie's small private income, Gladys found it increasingly difficult to buy food and run both the inn and the Mission on the small payments made by the visiting muleteers. However, her financial problem was solved when she received a most unusual request from the local Mandarin (a Chinese official of high rank). One day, he called at the inn and told Gladys, 'I have come about your feet. I have come for your help because you have *big* feet.' Gladys was astonished.

'But what can *I* do, Mandarin?' she asked.

'Will you become the Inspector of Feet?' he replied. 'The government will provide a mule and two soldiers to accompany you. You will receive a small salary—a measure of millet a day and a farthing to buy vegetables.'

Slowly, it dawned on Gladys what he was asking. For centuries, Chinese mothers had observed the custom of binding their daughter's feet from babyhood. In consequence, Chinese women grew up with feet that were fashionably small, but so stunted that normal walking was very difficult. A new government had decreed that this ancient practice was to cease.

Gladys saw the opportunities that such an appointment would give her. She agreed to the Mandarin's proposal on condition that she would be allowed to talk to the women about her religion and to preach unhindered in the villages she would visit. Gladys soon became known not only as the government's Inspector of Feet but also as 'The Storyteller'. Gradually, a few people were won over to the Christian Faith and in each village a small group gathered together to form the nucleus of a Church.

Although she was always busy, Gladys often felt isolated and lonely. She longed for someone to come out from England to share in her work; but no-one came. One day when she was feeling particularly depressed, she came across a woman sitting by the roadside with her small daughter. The child was thin, dirty and covered with sores. Gladys expressed concern for her; the mother replied by offering to sell the child for half a crown. Gladys was outraged and went immediately to the Mandarin to protest. But because the sale of young children was generally accepted, he could take no action. Gladys returned to the woman and, after some bargaining, gave her all the money she possessed at the time, five Chinese coins, roughly the equivalent of ninepence in (pre-decimal) English coinage. She therefore named the little girl 'Ninepence'. Gladys now had someone of her own to love and care for. A few months later, Ninepence brought in a small boy from the streets; he later brought two more, and before long, Gladys found herself caring for twenty unwanted children.

The people of the province grew to love Gladys; they said, 'She is one *of us*.' To make that beyond doubt, she destroyed her British passport and applied to become a naturalised Chinese subject. The Mandarin, a cultured, well-educated man, became a good friend with whom she often discussed religion. One day he paid her the highest of compliments.

'You are a great figure in my province, Ai-weh-deh,' he

said. 'You care for the sick; you help at child-birth; you visit our criminals; you mother our unwanted children. In every lonely village, in every part of the mountains, you are welcome; yet you come to us as a stranger and a foreigner. This must be a very strong faith of yours, Ai-weh-deh.'

In July 1937, China became involved in war with Japan. One morning, in the Spring of 1938, the people of Yangcheng heard the drone of aeroplanes overhead. But it was not until a series of shattering explosions rocked the town that its citizens realised that they were being bombed by the Japanese. One bomb struck a corner of the roof of the Mission-house where Gladys and her 'staff' were gathered for morning prayers. She was knocked out, and only regained consciousness as she was dragged from the rubble.

The Chinese townsfolk were too shocked to cope with the situation and as soon as Gladys had regained her senses she took command. She went calmly through the streets, helping the wounded and giving orders for the rescue of those trapped in the ruined buildings. She seemed to be the one person who knew what to do, and even the soldiers obeyed her instructions.

From this time on, Yangcheng was at the centre of the fighting. Four times the city changed hands. Each time that the Japanese occupied it, the people fled to the hills and found shelter in caves and holes in the ground, only returning when the Chinese troops re-captured it. One day, the Mandarin came looking for Gladys. He found her in one of the caves caring for a group of frightened refugees. He told her that he was leaving the province and had come to say farewell.

'I have watched you ever since you came, Ai-weh-deh,' he said. 'You love all our people, and you work hard for them.'

'It is God's will that I do so, Mandarin,' she replied.

'That I have come to know,' he said. 'Before I leave, I would like to be received into your Church and worship the God you worship. Will you grant this?'

'*God* will grant it, Mandarin,' Gladys replied, her eyes full of tears. The Mandarin was one of her most eminent converts.

As the war dragged on, Gladys had more and more children thrust upon her. Soldiers and villagers came to her with war-orphans and sick, neglected little waifs. Sometimes children came to the Mission on their own, having been told that they would find shelter there. Soon Gladys had over a hundred children in her care. They needed constant attention, and it became increasingly difficult to beg food for them and for the other refugees who crowded into the Mission. In addition, many wounded soldiers were brought to Gladys for medical aid, and the courtyard was often turned into a field-dressing station.

Gladys felt a growing concern for the safety of the refugee children. She heard that Madame Chiang Kai-shek had opened a number of orphanages in the unoccupied western provinces. It was decided that Mr Lu should take a party of a hundred children to the orphanage at Sian in the province of Shensi.

Within a month of their departure, however, Gladys found herself caring for a hundred *more* homeless children. Yet, in spite of this daunting task, she still found time to visit her Christian converts in the neighbouring villages. These visits also enabled her to assist the Chinese Nationalist Army by supplying valuable information concerning Japanese troop movements in the area.

Early in the Spring of 1940, the General in command of the Chinese troops defending the neighbouring city of Tsechow sent a message to Gladys warning her of his imminent withdrawal. He offered an escort to take her and the children to safety. Gladys let him take the children, but refused to go herself. 'Christians never retreat,' she said. The General sent another soldier to plead with her to leave. He showed her a poster issued by the Japanese, offering a reward for information leading to the capture of three individuals. Gladys read the names; one of those wanted was, 'The Small Woman, known as Ai-weh-deh.'

She told the messenger that she needed time to think and pray, and he departed without her. By the next morning she had decided to go. To her dismay, she discovered that the Japanese were already surrounding Yangcheng. She crept out of a small back-gate in the city walls and ran for her life. Some of the enemy soldiers spotted her and opened fire. Their bullets splattered all around her; she stumbled, fell, struggled to her feet and ran on and on until the firing ceased and she was safe. The next day, she reached Cheng Tsuen, a town still held by the Chinese Nationalists. There she found her children waiting anxiously for her.

She decided that these children must not remain any longer in the war-zone. She proposed to take them herself to the safety of Sian. Her friends tried to dissuade her, arguing that she had neither food nor money, and Sian was a very long distance away. Furthermore, because the Japanese army controlled the roads, she would have to travel on foot across steep, rugged mountains. Characteristically, she replied, 'The Lord will provide.'

Early the next morning she set out with an excited crowd of a hundred children, whose ages ranged from under three to sixteen. The older children helped the smaller ones, often carrying them on their backs. They begged for food as they went, and sang hymns and choruses to keep up their spirits.

For twelve weary days and shivering nights they trudged on until at last they caught a glimpse below of the Yellow River, glittering in the sun. When they reached its banks their hearts sank; there was no ferry and no other means of crossing. Gladys was exhausted and near to despair. All that night she lay awake worrying, and praying for guidance.

When dawn broke, Sualon, a girl of thirteen, came to her and asked her a question: if God had enabled Moses and the Israelites to cross the Red Sea on dry land, surely he would do the same for them? This shook Gladys.

'But I am not Moses,' she gasped.

'Of course you're not,' the girl replied, 'but Jehovah is still God.'

Gladys had no answer to this; ashamed of her lack of faith, she said, 'All right, we *will* go across.'

Sualon called some of the older children together and led them in a simple prayer, 'Here we are, Lord, just waiting for you to open up the Yellow River for us.'

Silently, Gladys prayed, 'O God, I am finished. I can do nothing more. I am at the end. . . . O God, don't let us down. Save us—prove yourself.'

Just then, some of the smaller boys ran up accompanied by a Chinese army officer. He warned them that a Japanese attack was expected at any moment, but he promised to try to obtain a boat to take them across. He was as good as his word, and soon all the children were safely on the other side. They made their way into a small town where the people took the children into their own homes and fed them.

They had already walked about sixty miles, but Sian was approximately another two hundred and fifty miles away. After a few days rest, they set off for Mien Chow; there they joined a train crowded with refugees. After four days travel, they came to a halt at Tiensan—a railway bridge had been destroyed and the train could go no further.

With two Chinese soldiers to escort them, Gladys and the children made a nightmare journey on foot over another mountain range, arriving after three days at Tung Kwan. There were no passenger trains running from there, either, but a sympathetic official told them to climb on to the trucks of a coal train heading for Sian. As the train ran close to the Japanese lines and was liable to be fired on, the children hid among the large lumps of coal. They travelled through the night, arriving at Hwa Chow black with coal dust, but unharmed. After waiting for several days, they were able to board another train which took them the last sixty miles to Sian. They marched joyfully from the station, only to find that the city was already so over-crowded with refugees that the gates were closed against them.

Gladys wept with disappointment and fatigue; she had driven herself nearly to the point of collapse. She was not to be beaten, however, and when she was informed that there was another of Madame Chiang's orphanages further on at Fu Feng, she encouraged her exhausted children to make one last effort. It was a day's journey by rail; but this time, when they arrived, they received a warm welcome and soon food and beds were made ready for them. They had set out in March, it was now late

April. For Gladys it had been an enormous test of faith and courage. She thanked God again and again that he had led them at last to safety.

The long trek accomplished, Gladys was at a loss to know what to do with herself. However, the day after they arrived, two Chinese women invited her to go with them to visit a Christian household in a village nearby. It had been intended that she should preach a short sermon, but as they sat down for a meal, Gladys collapsed. A doctor was called who diagnosed a lethal combination of relapsing fever, typhus, pneumonia, malnutrition and exhaustion. He held out little hope of her recovering; but when they were able to move her to a hospital in Sian, the doctors and nurses fought a desperate battle to save her life.

It was six months before she began to show any marked physical improvement, and two years before her mind was properly clear. She was still not fully recovered when, at her own insistence, she resumed work. She moved from town to town, mainly engaged in relief work among the hundreds of refugees who had fled from the war zone. She took every opportunity there was to preach, even going into a Buddhist monastery to explain Christianity to the five hundred lamas who lived there.

Eventually, she settled in Chengtu, where she commenced visiting a leper colony and a prison—the second largest in China. Each day, standing on a mound of earth in the prison exercise yard, she preached to the inmates. The conversion of a notorious murderer led to something of a religious revival there. Her influence was such that the prison Governor called her in to quell a riot. One of the prisoners was running amok with a hatchet, other prisoners were fighting each other. Gladys waded into the thick of the battle, demanded the hatchet and then scolded them all for 'being so silly'.* The Governor, convinced by the change in even the hardest criminals, became a Christian, testifying that what he had been unable to do for

*Alan Burgess places this incident during Gladys's second year in Yangcheng. The chronology of Gladys Aylward's 'Personal Story as Told to Christine Hunter' is followed here.

them in five years of penal correction, the power of Christ had accomplished in a few months.

When the Methodist Church in Chengtu advertised for an evangelist to deal with the refugees who were then pouring into the city, Gladys applied. She was appointed with permission to continue her visitation of the prison and the leper colony. There were many conversions in the district in spite of the fact that the Christian community now faced a sinister new threat from the Communist party who were gradually gaining power throughout China. In Chengtu they took complete control of the University, and two hundred Christian students who refused to renounce their Faith were publicly beheaded. Gladys herself was black-listed by the Communists as a subversive influence.

By this time, Gladys had been in China for seventeen years and she felt torn between staying in the land she had grown to love and returning home to see her ageing mother. It was with considerable heartache that, in the Spring of 1949, she set sail for England. She describes how she felt on her return: 'I had gone to China with very little except youthful determination. I came back, middle-aged, with absolutely nothing but the know-ledge that God had never failed me. Maybe I would find many things strange and difficult, but if God had work for me here, He would supply all that was necessary and lead me a step at a time.'

The next twenty years were spent preaching, and speaking about her experiences in China. At first she remained unknown, but in the Autumn of 1949, BBC Radio broadcast a half-hour dramatisation of her story in the series, 'The Undefeated'. She became famous overnight. The story of her life became still more widely known when the book, *The Small Woman*, was published in 1957. She was persuaded to grant a film company the rights to dramatise the book, a decision she lived to regret.

All this time, Gladys longed for the East, and when her mother died, she felt free to return. But China was now Mao Tse-tung's Peoples' Republic and was closed to her. Con-sequently, in April 1957, she sailed for Hong Kong. There, with the help of one of her 'children', now a grown man, she established a little Mission in the refugee area of the city. As she could not obtain a visa to stay in Hong Kong, she moved on to Formosa, an island off the coast of the mainland, now known as Taiwan, the seat of the Chinese Nationalist Government.

Arriving in the Autumn of 1957, she stayed for six years, preaching, acting as an interpreter, and caring for abandoned babies and homeless children. She rented an old hotel on the outskirts of Taipei which became known as the 'Gladys Aylward Orphanage'; she soon had a hundred children in her care—just as in her former days in Yangcheng.

To arouse interest and secure financial support for her work, she made a number of speaking tours of the USA, Canada, Australia and other major nations. The only shadow over her life during this period of intense activity was the release of the film, 'The Inn of the Sixth Happiness'. The film-makers had added a fictional romance to her life-story which caused Gladys acute embarrassment and sadness.

In March 1963, she was brought back to London by air and found herself the subject of the BBC Television programme, 'This Is Your Life'. She was surprised that she should be considered important enough to be featured in such a programme. She was even more surprised when, a few days later, she was invited to Buckingham Palace to lunch with Queen Elizabeth II and Prince Philip.

When the lease on the old hotel in Taipei expired, a more suitable house was acquired which became the new 'Children and Babies Home'. Gladys was now assisted in running it by Kathleen Langton Smith, a former postmistress from Nottingham who had volunteered her help. Their work was supported with funds raised in Britain by the Gladys Aylward Charitable Trust.

Gladys made her last visit to England in 1966, returning to Taiwan early in the new year. She had no thought of retiring and during the last two years of her life she was as busy as she had ever been. She was a popular visitor at the U.S. Base on Tapei and in constant demand as a speaker. In January 1970, she was booked to give a talk at a New Year meeting of the women of the Base. The weather was damp and cold. Gladys was still recovering from influenza but insisted on fulfilling her engagement. She returned very tired and feverish, and went early to bed. A doctor was called who found that the influenza had developed into pleurisy. That same night she died peacefully in her sleep.

Her funeral service in Taipei was attended by over a thousand people, and memorial services were held in many cities in England, Australia, New Zealand and America. She was buried on a hill that faces across the sea to the mainland of China, looking in the direction of Yangcheng, the city of which she went first when God 'had taken her on'.

ACKNOWLEDGEMENTS

This chapter is based on the books cited below, with grateful acknowledgement to their Authors and Publishers.

For Further Reading

'The Small Woman': Alan Burgess: Evans Brothers Ltd, 1957: Pan Books Ltd, 1959

'Gladys Aylward—Her personal story as told to Christine Hunter': Moody Bible Institute, 1970; Coverdale House Publishers Ltd, 1971

'A London Sparrow—the story of Gladys Aylward': Phyllis Thompson: Word (UK) Ltd, 1971; Pan Books Ltd, 1972

'Single Ticket to China'—Faith in Action Series: Douglas Hare: R E P, 1974

'Girl Friday to Gladys Aylward': Vera Cowie; Lakeland Press, 1976.

Filmstrip

'The Life of Gladys Aylward' (Ref. C 6492): Educational Productions Ltd, Bradford Road, East Ardsley, Wakefield, Yorkshire, WF3 2JN

Film

'The Inn of the Sixth Happiness' (contains an element of fiction): Film Distributions Associated (16 mm) Ltd, Building No. 9, GEC Estate, East Lane, Wembley, Middlesex, HA9 7QB

CHAPTER TWO

Artist Without Hands

John Buchanan

Born 1908

John Buchanan was born without hands. Instead, he had two
imperfectly formed fingers where his left hand should have
been, and his right arm finished with a stump at the elbow.
Soon after his birth in Glasgow in 1908, his family moved to a
village near Portsmouth where John spent his early days. Life
was not easy. His father had lost a leg in the Boer War and
found it hard to obtain and keep a job. It was an arduous task for
John's mother to look after her four other children and to give
her crippled son the extra attention he needed.

Prospects for John seemed bleak. It was suggested that he
should be taken into the care of the National Children's Home.*
Before accepting him, a medical examination was required.
This was conducted by a prominent Harley Street physician who
said in his report to the Home: 'Here is a lad who in all prob-
ability will never be able to earn his own living. If you take him
at all, take him for just a year on trial. His disability may be
more than you can cope with.'[1] The National Children's Home
were prepared to take the risk and John was admitted when he
was nine years old and sent to the Branch for Crippled Children
at Chipping Norton. He settled down quickly and early reports
referred to him as an intelligent, likeable youngster who was

* The National Children's Home founded by Dr Stephenson in 1869 comes
under the auspices of the Methodist Church. It provides an effective voluntary
child care organisation of Homes, Schools and Family Help in England,
bridging the areas of need not provided for in the modern welfare state.

'particularly nice to other children'. His sense of humour and cheerfulness soon made him a favourite with everyone.

John took part in all the activities of the Home's Open Air School. To everyone's surprise he began to show unusual promise as an artist. Although it had seemed unlikely that John would ever hold as much as a pencil, he discovered a way of holding a pen or brush between the stumps of his arms, and began to produce work which would have been a credit to any child with normal hands.

John was full of energy and determined to be as independent as possible. He became a Boy Scout, and when the day came for him to take his 'Tenderfoot' Test, the Scoutmaster decided that, in view of John's disability, he should be allowed to pass if he managed to tie just one of the six knots usually required. John refused the offer, 'No fear!' he said, 'I don't want my badge till I've earned it. I won't take it if I can't tie the whole lot.' He passed!

It was not long before he became the Editor of the *Magazine of the Handicapped Troop*. In addition to his work as editor, he designed the cover, cut the stencil and wrote out the original material for duplication. The more difficult the task, the harder he tried. Typical was the way in which he learned to knit by having corks fixed on the end of each knitting needle which he could then grip under his arms.

To develop his artistic ability, John was enrolled at the City of Oxford School of Art. The physical strain of travelling daily from Chipping Norton was considerable and one evening a Sister of the Children's Home found him alone in a mood of deep depression. At her words of sympathy John broke down and wept, saying that he 'should never have been allowed to live'.

Because of his frustrating handicap it was inevitable that, as he grew up, there should be periods of dejection. However, the mood passed and he began to plan for an independent future. While at the Oxford School of Art he was given money to buy a mid-day meal. Instead of having a proper lunch he usually bought himself a cup of tea and a bun, putting the money thereby saved into a box, as an insurance for his future. One of the Sisters, who had much to do with his early training, declared that

> 'John Buchanan's greatest victory was over himself. He knew his own weaknesses, was always free in admitting them, and made heroic efforts to overcome them. He had aspirations which far outran his powers of accomplishment, but because of those aspirations his achievements reached and remained on an amazingly high level.' [2]

It soon became clear that John's particular talent was the illumination of literary quotations. He became adept at lettering and tracery; he had a wonderful sense of colour and displayed great originality in the design of border and background. While still at Chipping Norton he bought large, plain postcards on which he wrote texts or mottos in colour. He sent them to a Sister of the National Children's Home who was living in London, and she sold them for him. At first they sold for three (old) pence each, but as his skill increased his work began to fetch a good price, and his reputation spread.

At the age of seventeen, John did some work which captured the attention of the late Lord Montagu of Beaulieu. The result was a commission to copy extracts of the ancient Deeds relating to Beaulieu Abbey. John's work was hung on the walls of the Abbey library. In 1926, he achieved outstanding success in a Competition for Industrial Design organised by the Royal Society of Arts. His work was exhibited at the Imperial Institute and won First Prize in the class for Pottery and Glass. Many of his designs received awards at the Exhibition, although neither the judges nor the Director of the Society knew until later of John Buchanan's handicap. The following year he received a commission from the late Queen Mary to paint some Christmas cards. This led to other work being done for the then Prince of Wales and other distinguished people. His work was so beautiful that it continually excited the admiration of those who saw it, whether they knew of his disability or not.

By this time he was working in a studio at Highbury, London.

Requests for a wide variety of work began to arrive in ever-increasing numbers and soon John was fully self-supporting. One of his most beautiful pieces of work was the illumination of a book which described a newly formed Ladies' Association of the National Children's Home. The book bears the autograph of her Royal Highness the Princess Royal and has been the means of introducing many people to the work of the Home. On one occasion, Cecil F. Walpole—then General Secretary of the National Children's Home—was showing the book to Lady Lucy. She was thrilled with its colour and beauty, and said, 'If, Mr Walpole, you can help a crippled lad like this to do so much, there must be lots of others who should be given a similar chance. Here is a cheque for a thousand pounds. Start a Scholarship Fund with it, and may many be helped by it.'

Another splendid example of John's artistry is to be seen in the Nurses' War Memorial Scroll in the Cathedral of St James, Liverpool. However, he became more widely known through his designs for calendars and greetings cards, which were reproduced by the million. John played his own part in the War effort, 1939-1945. The Admiralty sponsored a series of Warship Weeks and offered to present to each parish which reached a target of National Savings, a certificate endorsed with the name of the parish, the ship adopted, and the week in which the money was contributed. John did the bulk of this work, completing over 3,500 certificates in less than twelve months.

John never forgot his indebtedness to the National Children's Home. When the Home formed the 'League of Light' for fundraising, he was asked to design an attractive collecting box. He produced a box in the form of a lantern. These little lanterns have been used all over the country and have been the means of raising thousands of pounds a year for the work of the Home.

Although John Buchanan won the friendship of many eminent people, his deepest friendship was made when spending a holiday at Alverstoke, a branch of the Children's Home on the south coast. Sister Jane, a young child-care worker on the staff, helped John with the one task which, in spite of his amazing independence, he never learned to do on his own—to put on his necktie! Sympathy and affection developed into love, and their marriage and subsequent adoption of a baby girl, brought to John a happiness that he had scarcely dared to hope might be his.

John Buchanan was one of those people who did not talk much about his religion, but lived it. His faith was manifest in many ways. He had an unfailing sense of values. In his work he aimed at perfection; his chief motivation was not so much to earn a living but to create that which was worthwhile and beautiful. His love of God was expressed in love for his fellow men and women. It is said of him that: 'he was generous in his thoughts of others and still more in his actions'.[3] In strict confidence he gave liberally to any who needed help and was friend to many who were in personal difficulty. The way in which he overcame his own severe limitations was an inspiration, especially to those who were seriously handicapped themselves. Cecil F. Walpole, in his memoir of John Buchanan, recalls how he had told John that his life and example had helped people of all kinds, and asked him if he minded his name being mentioned in public. Quietly, he replied,

'Mr Walpole, I don't know why people should wish to know about me for there is so little I have really been able to do. If, however, you really think that my story can be of help to anyone, then you are free to talk about me in any way you like. God has always been good to me, and if there is anything I can do to show my gratitude to Him, then I want to do it.'[4]

John's whole outlook was coloured by his Christian attitude to life. Evidence of this can be seen during the days at Chipping Norton when he sent a gift to a sportsman whom he greatly admired. The sportsman was Jack Hobbs, the famous Surrey and England cricketer, one of the world's finest batsmen. John sent him a card inscribed with beautifully illuminated lettering. The words were from *Alumnus Football* by Grantland Rice:

And when the One Great Scorer comes
To write against your name,

He marks—not that you won or lost—
But how you played the game

Like many others with severe handicaps, John had a heightened sense of gratitude for the kindness and help shown to him by all kinds of people. During the last two years of his life he spent much of his time in hospital. He was particularly grateful to Mr Pennybacker, the surgeon who operated on him. In a letter to a friend, John wrote, 'I am speechless when I consider his nerve and skill, which has given me a fresh lease of usefulness. I have written a letter of thanks to him personally as, although I can render thanks by working again, I would like him to know of my gratitude. . . . For all the blessings of home, health, and work I thank God!'[5]

Many people have been helped and encouraged by his life and example. For instance, a distinguished Harley Street physician, who had been sent one of John's coloured calendars, wrote to the Secretary of the National Children's Home referring to a baby he was treating who had been born without arms. At first, the mother of the baby was desperate and hopeless, but gradually she came to a more positive frame of mind. The physician wrote, 'I have sent her your calendar, and it has helped her very much, as showing how very well cripples often can and do overcome their handicaps.' He stressed the 'great happiness and encouragement' that it had brought her.[6]

On 12 January 1953, at the age of forty-five, John Buchanan died. At his funeral the Reverend John W. Waterhouse, then Principal of the National Children's Home, paid tribute to John's skill, generosity and courage. He said:

'It was because John Buchanan had seen a vision of the purpose of the Great Artificer that he was able to design things of such beauty and meaning. His skill was thus linked with his faith, which was simple but profound. This skill was not acquired without years of striving towards the goal that was set before him, and in this connection unstinted praise must be given to his courage which enabled him to overcome great physical disability with cheerfulness. A lesser man might have given in to a life of dependence on others, but John Buchanan never let circumstance gain the mastery over him. He moulded his own way of life and it was an example to all.'[7]

The quality of John's work—his delicate traceries, his imaginative use of colour, his originality of design and his exactness in lettering—has evoked world-wide acknowledgement. His character made an equal impression on those who knew him personally. The saying, *Character is the measure of the things one has overcome*, is particularly applicable to his life. Cecil F. Walpole concludes his memoir of John Buchanan,

'His work added much beauty to the world: his life added more. This handless artist stood for something pure and enduring and, when the end came, he left the world better for his having passed through it.'[8]

For Further Reading

'Artist Without Hands': Cecil F. Walpole: Epworth Press, 1953 (Out of Print: but should be available from a local library)

Reference

Grateful acknowledgement is made to the Author and Publisher of the book cited below:

1. 'Artist Without Hands': p. 16.   2. Ibid, p. 25.   3. Ibid, p. 42.
4. Ibid, p. 40.   5. Ibid, p. 43.   6. Ibid, p. 46.   7. Ibid, p. 48.
8. Ibid, p. 48.

Films

Films about the work of the National Children's Home. (These and other films are available from the address below)

'A Century of Caring': made for the centenary in 1969 of the N.C.H. Tells the story of the Home's work from its foundation. Col. 45 mins.

'Today's Children': shows why it is still necessary after a hundred years for the N.C.H. Covers many different types of work in child care.

'Life Is What You Make It': an account of the work of the Penhurst School, Chipping Norton which John Buchanan attended. The school cares for children with a wide variety of handicaps. Col.

'Children in the Picture': shows the facilities and care provided for physically handicapped children at Elmfield and also features the adjoining branch, Highfield in Hertfordshire. Col. 15 mins.

'They Can Be Helped': a film about multi-handicapped children featuring four children at the N.C.H. day care pre-school unit at Ebley, near Stroud. Col.

For Further Information and hire of Films

The National Children's Home: 85 Highbury Park, London N5 1UD, who publish a quarterly magazine 'Children'

CHAPTER THREE

Love is a Fruit Always in Season

Mother Teresa

Born 1910

Calcutta, the largest city in India, sprawls over 270 square miles. The population of Greater Calcutta is more than 7,000,000 and still growing. At least 400,000 people in the city are homeless, and a high proportion of the others live in appalling slum conditions. Starvation, malnutrition, disease and poverty are rife. Men, women and children can be seen dying on the streets. In the midst of this scene of human need stands a long, white-washed building; a board at the entrance carries the inscription:

Corporation of Calcutta

NIRMAL HRIDAY

Home for Dying Destitutes

Nirmal Hriday—the Place of the Pure Heart, the home where the doors are always open. There are two rooms in the house, each containing seventy-two beds. The men and women in them have been carried there from the streets unconscious or semi-conscious. Half of them die within a few hours of their arrival, but here, at least, they die in peace and with some semblance of dignity. There are now many other such homes for the dying poor, not only in India but in numerous other countries too. They all owe their origin to one woman—Agnes Gonxha Bojaxhiu, now known throughout the world as Mother Teresa.

Agnes, one of three children of Albanian parents, was born

on 27 August 1910, in Skopje, Yugoslavia. Although there was no religious instruction at the state school which she attended, Agnes grew up a devout Roman Catholic. Whilst still at school she became a member of Sodality (an association for prayer and charitable action). She was only twelve years old when she became sure that she had a vocation to serve the poor. At that time a group of Yugoslav Jesuits had begun work in Calcutta. One of them was sent to Kurseong, and from there sent enthusiastic letters about the Bengal mission field. These letters were read to the Sodalists. Agnes determined that when she was older, she would volunteer to go to India as a missionary teacher. At first she had not wished to become a nun, but when she was eighteen, she decided to leave home and enter the Loreto teaching Order. She was accepted as a postulant in 1928 and sent for training to the mother-house of the order at Rathfarnham, Dublin, in Ireland. From there she went to India to begin her novitiate in Darjeeling. Her first vows were taken in 1931, her final vows in 1937. Between 1929 and 1948, she taught geography at St Mary's High School in Calcutta. For some years she was Principal of the school and was also in charge of the Daughters of St Anne, the Indian religious order attached to the Loreto Sisters.

She enjoyed teaching, but became increasingly troubled by the vast difference between the comfort and tranquillity of the convent school and the conditions of abject poverty in which thousands of Indian peasants lived. For Sister Agnes, 10 September 1946 proved to be a day of decision. As she travelled by train to Darjeeling for her annual retreat, she heard the call of God to serve him among the 'poorest of the poor' in the slums of Calcutta. She could not, however, change her work as a teacher without permission from the authorities of her order, to whom she had promised total obedience. This permission was slow in coming, and it was two years before she was allowed to leave the convent and become an 'unenclosed' nun.

On 8 August 1948 she laid aside the habit worn by the nuns of the Loreto order and, for four rupees, purchased a simple white cotton sari with a blue border; on one shoulder she fastened a small cross. She then went to Patna for three months of intensive nursing training under the American Medical Missionary Sisters. On 18 December 1948 she returned to Calcutta and found a place to live in the worst slums of the city. Three days later she started an open-air school in Moti Jheel. On the first day five children came and she began by giving each of them a much needed wash. Numbers increased rapidly, and soon she was glad to receive the help of some of the women teachers from her former convent school.

Although constantly surrounded by people who were hungry, diseased and poverty-stricken, she was particularly saddened by the sight of those who lay dying on the pavements. One day, with no clear-cut plan in mind, she went over to where there lay the filthy, emaciated body of a woman, already half eaten by rats and ants. The woman had lost so much weight that Mother Teresa was able to pick her up and carry her in her arms to the local hospital. There was nothing that the hospital could do for the woman, but they took her in because the determined-looking little nun who had brought her refused to move until they did.

There were so many others dying uncared-for that Mother Teresa felt utterly inadequate to do anything effective for them. But help came—first, from Michel Gomes, a state administration official, who gave her a room on the top floor of a house he owned. She moved in during February 1949, and brought there a few of the worst cases that no hospital would admit. Then, on 19 March, she was joined by one of her former pupils at the school, a pretty, well-to-do Bengali girl named Subhasini Das, who arrived and said, 'I want to become one of your Sisters.' Soon other young girls came to volunteer their assistance. The first nine, like Subhasini, were all former students of St Mary's, where Mother Teresa had taught for twenty years. So a new Congregation of Sisters, The Missionaries of Charity, came into being with the blessing of the Pope. The motherhouse was founded on 7 October 1950 at 54A Lower Circular Road, Calcutta 16. To the usual vows of poverty, chastity and obedience, there was a fourth vow required of the Missionary

Sisters of Charity, namely: 'To serve the poorest of the poor of all classes and creeds . . . to recognise God in the person of the poor, the unwanted, the unloved.'

Mother Teresa had commenced her work in the slums with only five rupees. However, as more people heard about what she and the Sisters were doing, they began to donate money and equipment. As the Order grew, other helpers—among them doctors and nurses—came to give their services on a part-time, voluntary basis. The house of Mr Gomes was now too small for the large numbers of the sick and dying that Mother Teresa brought there. The health officer of the municipality offered her two rooms attached to the Temple of Kalighat, which was dedicated to the Hindu goddess Kali. Here a 'Home for the Dying' was opened in 1954; only the most desperate cases whom no hospital would treat were taken in. Typical was an old man found in a ditch; he was just a bundle of skin and bone, barely alive. Mother Teresa washed him and made him comfortable. Shortly before he died, the old man muttered, 'all my life I have lived like a beast, and now I am dying like a human being. Why is this?' He died with his eyes focused on the cross pinned to Mother Teresa's sari.

Some years later, when interviewed on television by Malcolm Muggeridge, Mother Teresa summarised what she and the Sisters were seeking to do for the dying:

> 'First of all we want to make them feel that they are wanted, we want them to know that there are people who really love them, who really want them, at least for the few hours that they have to live, to know human and divine love. That they too may know that they are the children of God, and that they are not forgotten and that they are loved and cared about and there are young lives ready to give themselves in their service.' [1]

There are some who do not die. For those able to work, the Sisters attempt to find employment. They try to send the permanently disabled to homes where they can spend at least a few years of happiness in relative comfort.

In 1957, Mother Teresa extended her work to include those suffering from leprosy. This came about when five lepers arrived at the Nirmal Hriday asking for shelter. They had been thrown out of work and turned away from their own homes. Mother Teresa and the Sisters decided that the lepers needed treatment as well as shelter and food. In the next few weeks more lepers arrived seeking help. Fortunately, Dr Senn, a specialist in the treatment of leprosy, heard of Mother Teresa's predicament and offered his assistance in training the Sisters in the treatment of leprosy. Among the lepers who came were many well-educated, rich and capable people. Because of their disease they had been rejected by family, friends and society. Those who had held high positions in life were, like the rest, reduced to begging and forced to live in the slums unknown, unloved and uncared for.

Provided a leper comes in time for treatment, the new drugs now available are effective in arresting the progress of the disease. Just as important as medical care, is the moral support given by the Sisters, who seek to give back to their patients a sense of self-respect and dignity. Mother Teresa's guiding rule for this work is: 'Touch a leper, touch him with love.' To feel loved and accepted is of immense psychological value, especially to those whose faces, hands and feet are dreadfully disfigured by the ravages of the disease. The Sisters now have a special mobile clinic with which they visit eight leper colonies. They have also established three dispensaries to which thousands of lepers have come for treatment. From the time she began leprosy work, Mother Teresa saw the need for a settlement where, in addition to their medical treatment, the patients could be rehabilitated and educated. The government gave her thirty-four acres of land at Asansol, a site large enough to provide for the needs of 400 leper families. She trusted that God would provide the money required and made her plans for building what was to be called the City of Peace. On a visit to Bombay, Pope Paul VI presented her with his ceremonial car, a huge white American convertible. Mother Teresa organised a raffle with the car as the prize, and raised enough money to get her leper colony started.

The work of Mother Teresa and her Missionaries of Charity soon began to branch out in many new directions. She established maternity homes, orphanages and schools. In Calcutta, the children's home, 'Shishu Bhavan', takes in children as young as one day old who have been abandoned at birth. Among them there are many premature children whose lives have been saved by being placed in a home-made incubator, constructed by the Sisters from a packing case fitted with a powerful electric light bulb. Mother Teresa describes the circumstances in which children of all ages come to the Home:

> 'Many of those children are unwanted by their parents; some we pick up, some we get from hospital: they have been left there by their parents. Some we bring from jail, some are brought to us by the police. By whatever means they are brought to us, up to now we have never refused a child. . . . We always have one more bed for one more child.' [2]

Mother Teresa's work soon spread to most of the major cities of India and won widespread acclaim. In September 1962, she received the Padmashree Award from the President of India and also the Magsaysay Award for International Understanding given in honour of the late President of the Philippines. Further recognition of the Sisters came on 1 February 1965 when the Missionaries of Charity became a Society of Pontifical Right. Understandably, it is in Calcutta that there is their greatest concentration of activity. Thirty of their forty houses are situated there. By 1975 the number of Centres for medical and educational work had increased to fifty. There are at least 4,000 children in schools run by the Sisters in Calcutta. In addition, classes are held for adolescents and adults in typing, sewing and homecraft. The Centres also include joinery and metal workshops, a Family Planning Clinic and many clubs and co-operatives. Mother Teresa has ensured that the Society does not grow into a vast administrative institution by making a rule that all the Sisters, including the Superiors, must serve the poor for at least a part of *every* day. She writes most of her letters by hand and does her own clerical work when the other Sisters have gone to bed. She is also aware of the danger that the Missionaries of Charity could become simply social workers or merely do the work for its own sake. She says: 'It is a danger; if we forget to whom we are doing it. Our works are only an expression of our love for Christ. Our hearts need to be full of love for him and since we have to express that love in action, naturally then the poorest of the poor are the means of expressing our love for God . . . we do it to God, to Christ, and that's why we try to do it as beautifully as possible.'[3]   The Mass, prayer and meditation are an essential part of each day's programme. To Mother Teresa the need to withdraw, to be alone with God is as important as the work itself.

However, Mother Teresa does not retrict her helpers to those who are practising Christians. In Calcutta, many non-Christians work alongside the Sisters in the Home for the Dying and in the other Centres. Their common motivation is *love*, for as Mother Teresa says, *'Love is a fruit which is always in season.'*

Although a devout Roman Catholic, Mother Teresa has a wide-embracing attitude to other religious Faiths as is evident from her thoughts on conversion. She says,

> 'What we are all trying to do by our work, by serving the people, is to come closer to God. If in coming face to face with God we accept Him in our lives, then we are converting. We become a better Hindu, a better Muslim, a better Catholic, a better whatever we are, and then by being better we come closer and closer to Him. If we accept Him fully in our lives, then that is conversion. What approach would I use? For me, naturally, it would be a Catholic one, for you it may be Hindu, for someone else, Buddhist, according to one's conscience. What God is in your mind you must accept. But I cannot prevent myself from trying to give you what I have.'[4]

In the Chapel of the Missionaries of Charity, above the crucifix, there are written three words of Jesus spoken from the cross: 'I am thirsty.' Mother Teresa realises that in the face of mass poverty, disease and hunger, whatever they do is 'only one drop in an ocean of misery'. But, as she says, 'if that drop is not in the ocean I think the ocean will be less because of that missing drop; and each drop helps to assuage the thirst of Christ'. The Sisters seek to identify themselves with the poverty around them. Their list of possessions is small: two cheap saris, a pair of sandals, a piece of soap in a cigarette box, a metal bucket, one enamel plate and cutlery, a mattress and a thin coverlet. Their life is hard: they rise at 5 a.m. and work until 9 p.m., with only half an hour's rest during the day, and one day of rest during the week for meditation and reading; their food is plain and frugal. Nevertheless, in twenty-five years, the number of Sisters in the order has risen from five to well over nine hundred; the nuns come now from many nationalities.

With her field of action ever widening, it became apparent to Mother Teresa that certain tasks were too great for feminine strength alone. She therefore recruited nine young men who were willing to look after both the dying in the Nirmal Hriday, and the boys in her schools. On 25 March 1963 the Archbishop of Calcutta gave his official blessing to the establishment of a branch of the Missionary *Brothers* of Charity; Brother Andrew, an Australian Jesuit priest, became their first Superior.

By the end of 1975, there were one hundred and fifty brothers. Most of their work is in India, although five houses were opened in Vietnam and Cambodia to help war victims. Unfortunately, a change in the government of these nations necessitated the withdrawal of the Brothers. Their work in India is as comprehensive as that of the Sisters. It includes the provision of homes for dying destitutes, abandoned children and disabled people—including the mentally handicapped, leprosy and medical treatment, slum schools and youth clubs, projects for feeding the hungry, and disaster relief. Although they hope to start work again in the Far East, at the moment their only Congregation outside India is in Los Angeles, USA. There they work among alcoholics and destitutes, care for the elderly, and visit prisons and hospitals. A novitiate has now been opened and a few young Europeans have come to Los Angeles for training.

The work of Mother Teresa and her Sisters has had a world-wide impact. Requests to her to found branches of the Missionary Sisters of Charity have come from many countries. The first expansion outside India came in 1965, when a Bishop in Venezuela heard of their work in Calcutta, and appealed to Mother Teresa to help the poor in Caracas. Now there are three convents in Venezuela from which the Sisters go out daily to teach children, give lessons in homecrafts to adults, visit the sick, and take the Sacrament to those who have no priest. In December 1967, Mother Teresa visited Ceylon to open a House in Colombo. In August 1968, at the special request of the Pope, five Indian Sisters established themselves in one of the shanty-towns of Rome; helped by students the Sisters built their own house, showing considerable skill as bricklayers. The same year, the Sisters opened a Home for the Dying and a nursing centre in Tabora, Tanzania; and, at a request from the Government, they undertook to help care for some of the 14,000 refugees from Burundi. In October 1969, Mother Teresa established a settlement in Bourke which brought new hope and great benefit to the Aborigines of New South Wales, Australia.

A significant development was the formation of The International Association of Co-Workers of Mother Teresa. This was affiliated to the Order of the Missionaries of Charity on 26 March 1969, when its constitution received the blessing of Pope Paul VI. The Association 'consists of men, women, young people and children of all religions and denominations throughout the world who seek to love God in their fellow men through whole-hearted free service to the poorest of the poor of all classes and creeds, and who wish to unite themselves in a spirit of prayer and sacrifice with the work of Mother Teresa and the Missionaries of Charity'. There are now nearly 70,000 Co-Workers; they are to be found in many parts of the world; they are an invaluable means of support, providing food, clothing, money and publicity for work among the poor and needy.

In April 1970, Mother Teresa again visited Australia. She

established some of her Sisters in Melbourne where they opened a hostel for alcoholics and ex-prisoners, and where they also offered friendship and support to countless lonely and deprived people. A few months later, Mother Teresa was in Amman, Jordania, helping refugees and other victims of the six-day war. In doing this kind of work the lives of Mother Teresa and the Sisters are constantly in danger. For instance, during the crisis between the Jordanians and Fedayins, the Sisters' house was surrounded by Fedayin troops, who ordered the nuns to line up against a wall while they prepared to shoot them. Just in time a Moslem ran up and shouted, 'Stop! these nuns came to care for our poor people.' The Fedayins released them, apologising profusely. During the Indo-Pakistani conflict, Mother Teresa and her nuns took over responsibility for a huge Bengali refugee camp. With the end of hostilities in 1971, Sheikh Mujiba Rahman asked Mother Teresa to open three centres where the Sisters could care for some of the many hundreds of young women and girls violated during the civil war.

On 8 December 1970, Cardinal Heenan opened a centre in London to train novices from Europe and the Americas (this was transferred to Rome in August 1973). Two permanent hostels for destitutes have since been established in London. Mother Teresa was in England during the out-break of civil strife in Northern Ireland. 'There is an act of love to be done there', she said, and set up a centre in Belfast, which remained open until August 1973. The same year, she visited America. Having a special concern for the American negroes, she left five Sisters to work in the slums of Harlem, New York. Observing the life of these large cities has confirmed Mother Teresa's belief that: 'The biggest disease today is not leprosy or tuberculosis, but rather the feeling of being unwanted, uncared for and deserted by everybody. The greatest evil is the lack of love and charity, the terrible indifference towards one's neighbour who lives at the roadside assaulted by exploitation, corruption, poverty and disease.'[5]

On 6 January 1971, Mother Teresa received the Pope John

XXIII Peace Prize; the cheque for fifteen million lire was presented by Pope Paul VI, who said that it was right that in a world ravaged by hate and cruelty, attention should be drawn to a work of goodness and compassion. Mother Teresa was the first woman to receive this prize. She used the money to begin the 'Shanti dan' leprosy foundation at Raigahr, which is called 'The City of Peace'.

There has been a continual expansion of the activities of the Missionaries of Charity during the 1970s (see appendices). Mother Teresa is now an international figure who has received world-wide recognition for her work. The Pope John XXIII Peace Prize received in 1971 was only one of many such honours. She has been given several American awards, including the John F. Kennedy International Award (October 1971); she has also received the Pandit Nehru Award for International Understanding (November 1972), and the Templeton Foundation Prize for Progress in Religion. The latter was presented by H.R.H. Prince Philip, the Duke of Edinburgh, in London on 25 April 1973. In his presentation speech Prince Philip, said:

'The sheer goodness which shines through Mother Teresa's life and work can only inspire humility, wonder and admiration and what more is there to be said when the deeds speak so loudly for themselves? There is nothing I can say, dare say, about Mother Teresa, but I think there is much to be learned from her example. I believe the lesson we should learn on this occasion is a very simple one and a very old one. It is just that the strength of a person's faith is measured by his action.'

In March 1975, in 'tribute to Mother's exemplary love and concern for the hungry and the poorest of the poor', the United Nations Food and Agriculture Organisation struck its Ceres Medals with Ceres, the Roman goddess of agriculture, represented by Mother Teresa. Proceeds from the sale of the medals are being donated to the further work of the Missionaries of Charity.

Mother Teresa was also one of the recipients of the First Albert Schweitzer International Prizes awarded on 23 October 1975 at the University of North Carolina. On 2 November 1975 at the St Francis Xavier University, Nova Scotia, Canada honoured her by conferring on her an Honorary Degree of Doctor of Laws. On 16 June 1977, the Duke of Edinburgh, Chancellor of Cambridge University, conferred on her an Honorary Doctorate in recognition of her service to humanity.

Mother Teresa has received numerous other awards and honours; her attitude towards them is very simple. 'These are not for me,' she says, 'they are for my people. . . . It is the poor people who are being recognized. They are becoming wanted. Loved. The whole world is beginning to know about it.'[6]

The Silver Jubilee of the founding of the Missionaries of Charity was commemorated all over the world on 1 October 1975. Characteristically, Mother said, 'I want God to be the central figure in our celebration so that everyone's attention is drawn to God and all may acknowledge that it is His work and not ours—so no expense, no concerts, no decorations, only ''Thank You'' to God.'

The Jubilee celebrations which, in India, lasted for a week, illustrated the remarkable way in which the work of the Missionaries transcends all the usual barriers of caste, class and religion. In Calcutta, not only Christians, but Hindus, Buddhists and Muhammadans each held a special Thanksgiving Day. Each religious group organised a thanksgiving prayer service in their own place of worship and Mother went to share in each service at the appointed time, accompanied by different groups of the Sisters.

When, twenty-seven years earlier, Agnes Gonxha Bojaxhiu went alone to live in the slums of Calcutta, she could never have forseen that from such a small beginning would grow so great a movement of compassion. Mother Teresa is now in her sixties. When asked by a journalist if the time would ever come when she would slow down or retire, she laughed and replied, 'In the service of God there is no time for retirement; just eternal rest.' Many tributes have been paid to her, perhaps that of Malcolm Muggeridge comes nearest to the truth, 'For me', he said, 'Mother Teresa of Calcutta embodies *Christian love in action*. Her face shines with the love of Christ on which her whole life is centred, and her words carry the message to a world which never needed it so much.'[7]

The key to Mother Teresa's work and teaching is to be found in Christ's parable of The Sheep and the Goats (Matthew 25 vv. 31-45); she attaches particular significance to the words of Jesus: 'Inasmuch as you did it to the least of these my brethren, you did it unto me' (v. 40). Mother Teresa says, 'I see Christ in every person I touch because He has said, "I was hungry, I was thirsty, I was naked, I was sick, I was suffering. I was homeless and you took me in. . . . " It is as simple as that. Every time I give a piece of bread, I give it to Him.'[8]

She inspires her co-workers with this same spirit. A young man helping her at Nirmal Hriday was attending a destitute brought in from the street outside. As he dressed a gaping wound which was crawling with maggots, he was heard to say with genuine humility, 'When I cleanse the wounds of the poor, I am cleansing the wounds of Christ.'[9]

Mother Teresa is a missionary in every sense of the word; she is an evangelist, but not in the old propagandist manner. As Malcolm Muggeridge has said, 'She preaches Christ every moment of every day by living for and in him.'[10] She believes that her vocation is 'to belong to Jesus. Because I belong to Him, the work is a means for me to put love for Him into action. So it is not an end, it is a means.'[11]

Although deeply involved with death and suffering, she possesses a quiet joy; as she says, 'True holiness consists in doing God's will with a smile'; and, 'Let no-one ever come to you without coming away better and happier.' Malcolm Muggeridge describes the effect she had on an audience of ordinary people who had crowded into a school hall to hear her,

'Every face, young and old, simple and sophisticated, was rapt, hanging on her words; not because of the words themselves—they were ordinary enough—but because of her. Some quality that came across over and above the words held their attention. A luminosity seemed to fill the school hall, illuminating the rapt faces, penetrating into every mind and heart.' [12]

Mother Teresa believes that the way in which an act of kindness is done is as important as the action itself; she says, 'It is how much love we put in the doing that makes our offering "Something Beautiful for God".' To those who would serve Christ by serving the 'poorest of the poor', she says, 'Be the living expression of God's kindness: kindness in your face, kindness in your eyes, kindness in your smile, kindness in your warm greeting. In the slums we are the light of God's kindness to the poor, to all who suffer and are lonely, give always a happy smile. Give them not only your care, but also your heart.' [13] No-one exemplifies those words better than Mother Teresa herself; and nothing expresses better the purpose of her life than one of her own prayers:

Make us worthy, Lord, to serve our fellow-men through the world who live and die in poverty and hunger. Give them, through our hands, this day their daily bread, and, by our understanding, love, peace and joy.

APPENDIX I

Chronological Table of Events, January 1972 to December 1975

1972
New Foundations Opened:

January 21	Bangladesh
March 25	Novitiate in Melbourne, Australia
August 15	Convent in Mauritius

1973
New Foundations Opened:

February 26	Gaza, Israel
February 27	S. Vietnam—by the Brothers

March 25	Katherine, N.T. Australia
August 22	Hodeidah, the Yemen
August	Novitiate for Europe and the Americas transferred to Rome
September 18	Belfast Centre closed
October 4	Lima, Peru
November 23	Addis Ababa, Ethiopia

1974

New Foundations opened in India:

Shillong	Ernakulam
Guntakal	Bhubaneshwar
Vellore	Nägpur
Kettayam	

New Foundations outside India:

April 3	Phnom-Penh, Cambodia—by the Brothers
May 28	Greenvale, Australia
June 9	Palermo, Sicily
July 18	Papua New Guinea
August 11	Taiz, The Yemen
October 25	Tongi, Bangladesh

1975

New Foundations opened in India:

January 15	Berhampur, Orissa
January 21	'Prem Dan', Calcutta
January 27	Nonpoh, Meghalaya
January 31	'Prem Nivas', Jvotinagar, Lucknow
March 26	Hinoo
June 6	Raurkela, Orissa
June 13	Meerut
August 15	Maria Polli
September 7	Howrah
September 10	Ahmedabad, Gujarat
September 15	Dumka, Santal Paganas

New Foundations outside India:

| May 3 | Corpus Christi Home, Greenvale, Australia |
| June 6 | Naples |

1976

Foundations also established in Mexico City, Guatemala and Haiti

APPENDIX II

Summary of Statistics of the Missionary Sisters of Charity to 31 December 1975

1.	Foundations in India	60
	Outside India	27
2.	Professed	715
	Novices	316
	Postulants	196
3.	Schools	80
	No. of Children	8,181
4.	Adult Classes (Sewing)	88
	No. of girls	4,174
5.	Adult Classes (Commercial)	13
	No. of girls	299
6.	Homes for Abandoned Children	30
	Admissions	2,111
7.	General Dispensaries (Mobile Units)	314
	No. of patients	4,629,722
8.	Leprosy Clinics	75
	No. of patients	39,874
9.	Homes for Dying Destitutes	37
	Admissions	5,516
10.	Family Planning Centres	57
	No. of cases	8,323
11.	Relief Work—No. of families	24,243
12.	Sunday Schools	179
	No. of children	22,765

References

Grateful acknowledgement is made to the Authors and Publishers of 'Something Beautiful For God': Malcolm Muggeridge: Fontana, 1972 (SBFG); and 'Mother Teresa—Her People and Her Work': Desmond Doig: Collins; 1976 (MT)

1. SBFG p. 91   2. Ibid, p. 99f.   3. Ibid, p. 113f.   4. MT p. 156.
5. SBFG, p. 73.   6. MT, p. 151.   7. SBFG Rear Cover.   8. MT, p. 158.
9. Ibid, p. 145.   10. SBFG, p. 59.   11. MT, p. 158.   12. SBFG, p.126.
13. Ibid, p. 69.

For Further Reading

'Something Beautiful for God': Malcolm Muggeridge: W. Collins Sons & Co. Ltd, 1971, Fontana, 1972

'Mother Teresa and Calcutta': People With a Purpose Series: Sheila M. Hobden: SCM Press, 1973 (contains background information on India, and on Calcutta in particular)

'For the Love of God': Georges Gorrée and Jean Barbier: T. Shand Alba Publications, 1974

'A Gift for God—Prayers and Sayings of Mother Teresa': compiled by Malcolm Muggeridge: W. Collins Sons & Co. Ltd. 1975

'Mother Teresa—Her People and Her Work': Desmond Doig: William Collins Sons & Co. Ltd, 1976

'Mother Teresa': Christian Education Movement Leaflet 20: C.E.M., Annadale, Chester House, Pages Lane, London N10 1PR.

Films

'Mother Teresa of Calcutta': Oxfam, 1964. B/W. 15 mins

'Something Beautiful for God': Malcolm Muggeridge's interview for BBC TV, 1973. B/W. 50 mins

Both films available for hire from Concord Films Council Ltd, Nacton, Ipswich, Suffolk, IP10 OJZ. They and Film Strip/Slides 'Love without Frontiers' are also obtainable from Mrs. P. Bethell, The Small House, Cliftonville, Dorking, Surrey

For Further Information

The Co-workers of Mother Teresa in England: Hon. Secretary: Mrs. W. Noble, 'Fernhurst', East Road, St George's Hill, Weybridge, Surrey, KT13 0LD

CHAPTER FOUR

'When in Prison You Visited Me'*
John Dodd MBE

Born 1916

The Japanese Kempei Tai (Secret Police, similar to the German Gestapo) thought that he was a spy. Their ruthless questioning took place at a school they had taken over.

'Where your radio?' asked the interrogating officer.

'Haven't got one', John Dodd replied. 'Look,' he continued, 'I'm an RAF corporal. I was in Batavia when your blokes landed and I tried to get to Tjilatjap. I didn't make it and I've been on the run ever since. That's all.'

They did not believe him. The interrogation went on and on all that morning. At regular intervals he was knocked to the ground with the butt of a rifle and then kicked as he lay there.

By mid-day John was only semi-conscious. He was dragged outside to the school playground and made to stand in the blazing sun. Then three guards took it in turns to beat him. They used their rifles, their fists, their boots and a multi-thonged stockwhip.

The Kempei Tai were sure that he had friends who had hidden him while he was on the run, and the Japanese were determined to torture him until he revealed their identity. John was equally determined not to betray any of those who had helped him. His body was one mass of pain, and yet he experienced a curious sense of mental detachment. Through a mist of semi-consciousness his mind wandered back over the

* Matthew 25:36.

events that had led him to this time and place, standing where children used to play, being beaten—apparently to death.

Born in 1916, John had been brought up in Manchester where he attended the William Hulme Grammar School. He was intelligent, full of energy and good at sport. But, from his earliest years, he was a rebel against authority and, consequently, he had a difficult adolescence. Despite the persuasion of his teachers, he declined their advice to stay on at school in the sixth form, and looked for work as a sports writer on a local paper. The job did not materialize, so he then joined Shell Petroleum, but when he found that they required him to take a seven year course in pure chemistry, he left. Next, he worked for two years with a firm of estate agents, and eventually became a salesman, a job for which he seemed to have a natural flair.

At the outbreak of World War II, he joined the RAF. He was promoted to the rank of Corporal, and posted to the island of Singapore, arriving in July 1941. In November he was joined by his younger brother, Terry, who was also in the RAF.

By January 1942, the Japanese had fought their way down Malaya and, in February, were on the island of Singapore. John, along with the last of the Air Force personnel, was evacuated shortly before the invading army took the city itself. The over-crowded cargo vessel on which he sailed from Singapore was repeatedly bombed, and John narrowly escaped being killed in one of the raids. This was the first of a series of incidents from which he emerged safely while others died. At the time he thought that it was just his good luck; later, he was to put a different interpretation on his succession of escapes.

At last the damaged ship limped into Batavia (now Djakarta), the capital of Java. The port was in chaos. Invasion by the Japanese seemed a strong possibility and yet there were no official plans for evacuation. John decided to make the best of the situation. He made friends with a charming, well-educated woman, Marquita, and her teenage daughter, Phiphine, and they introduced him to an American pilot nicknamed Smudge.

Two weeks after John's arrival in Batavia, the Japanese

army landed on Java. Marquita, Phiphine, Smudge and John spent the next fortnight driving south, hoping to reach a port and find a boat to take them to Australia. With the Japanese army advancing all the time, their frantic search was like some hideous nightmare. Eventually, Smudge was captured and shot dead while trying to get away. On a number of occasions John himself avoided capture only because of Marquita's quick thinking and courage. The time came, however, when he realized that he must part company with the two women because his presence seriously endangered their lives.

It was decided that John should go into hiding in the jungle. Marquita and Phiphine were invited to stay in a small hut belonging to a sympathetic Dutch tea planter. Meanwhile, Marquita introduced John to some friendly Javanese, and their head-man, Ruslan, took him deep into the jungle and built him a hideout of bamboo and palm. After that, once a week, putting his own life at risk, Ruslan returned to John bringing him food and drink.

John was very lonely and terribly bored. The only book he had with him was a pocket New Testament which his mother had given him when he joined the RAF. She had asked him to read a few verses every day but he had never opened it. However, out of respect for his mother—who was a deeply religious woman—John had always carried it with him. Now it came in useful as he amused himself playing 'alphabet cricket'. He went through the New Testament word by word, using each letter of the alphabet to represent an incident in a make-believe game of cricket, thus a = one run, b = bowled, c = caught, and so on. He picked hypothetical teams, kept the score and, day after day, played imaginary Test matches.

At the end of six weeks, John felt that he could no longer stand his solitary existence. When Ruslan came on his weekly visit, John went back with him to where Marquita and Phiphine were staying. He had been with them only a few days, however, when he was nearly discovered by a Japanese search-party. He felt that he had no alternative but to return to the jungle; once more Ruslan accompanied him and built him another hut. As the days went by, John became deeply depressed; in fact, he believes that he would have gone insane but for a troop of monkeys who came to inspect him and with whom he gradually built up a kind of friendship.

That friendship was short-lived. After three weeks, John developed a severe fever and he was forced to return to Marquita and Phiphine. They nursed him with loving care and he began to recover. On the evening of the fourth day after his arrival back, he was alone in his room when the door crashed open, a torch shone in his eyes and he felt a bayonet pressed in his stomach. The Japanese had caught up with him at last. After a night of brutal questioning they took him to the school building recently occupied by the Kempei Tai. It was on the school playground that John now stood, more dead than alive, having endured four days of inhuman interrogation.

The next day, finding that they could not make him talk, the Japanese dumped him on the floor of a lorry and drove away from the school. After a few miles, they threw him out, tied his hands to the tail-board and dragged him behind the lorry. When he regained consciousness, John found himself in the makeshift hospital of a small prisoner-of-war camp in western Java. There, two Dutch doctors patched him up as best they could.

Later, he was taken to a grossly over-crowded gaol in Batavia. Day after day, he and hundreds of other prisoners were used as slave-labour, clearing rubble from the bomb-damaged docks. Many died from malnutrition and disease or from the brutal treatment they received from the Japanese guards. John survived, and after some weeks, was moved again. Following a terrible journey by rail and sea, he arrived back on the island of Singapore. It was almost a year since he had been evacuated from the island; now he was herded into the notorious Changi prison camp.

As a result of his beatings, John was badly scarred, nearly blind in his left eye, his kidneys were damaged and, like everyone else in that camp, he was suffering from dysentery. Some prisoners lost their will to live, but in spite of his poor physical condition, John was determined to survive. Moreover, his morale was given a great boost when he discovered that his brother, Terry, whom he had assumed had been killed when the Japanese invaded Singapore, was alive and in the same prison camp.

Life in Changi was a dreary round of work, hunger and brutality at the hands of the guards. Some prisoners, like Ernest Gordon*, learned how to overcome the mental and spiritual frustration of camp life. John, however, did not join any of the Christian groups which were formed nor did he attend the camp 'university' classes. He preferred to spend his time with the Australian prisoners. They spent their non-working hours gambling at cards or 'racing' bed bugs and frogs. Until it became too hazardous, John used his former skill as a salesman to sell cheap pens, watches and cigarette lighters to the Japanese guards, fooling them into thinking that they were buying high-quality articles. In this way, John and his fellow prisoners were able to supplement their meagre daily ration of rice.

Three years dragged by. Soon after Christmas 1944, John became seriously ill again and underwent an emergency operation. From his former thirteen stone he now weighed a mere six stone. One night a medical orderly called the camp doctor.

'I wish you'd have a look at Dodd, sir,' he said, 'he's very bad.'

'I can't understand why he's alive at all,' the doctor replied.

John overheard the conversation. 'I'll show him,' he thought to himself. Gradually, he did regain some strength and, by the end of June, he had put on half a stone in weight.

The last months of the war, John spent in the camp hospital. When Changi was liberated, he was parted from his Australian friends and his brother; while they were being repatriated, John was taken on a stretcher by hospital-ship and train for treatment at Bangalore. But, at least he was alive, and to have survived Changi was little short of a miracle. Before being sent home, John made strenuous efforts to discover whether Marquita and

* See chapter 6.

Phiphine were still alive. It was a hopeless task, and feeling helpless and bitter at the disappointment, he began the journey back to England.

His brother, Terry, was there to greet him on his arrival and escorted him to their parent's new home at Wootton Bridge on the Isle of Wight. Although John was thrilled to see his family again, coming home was nonetheless something of an anticlimax. There was a general air of disillusionment throughout the nation. People and places had changed and, like so many other ex-prisoners of war, John felt that somehow he did not 'fit in'. To add to his troubles, he had to undergo another operation. Nor was it encouraging when the surgeon told him afterwards that he would need further treatment and regular medical checks, probably for the rest of his life.

John's mother, a devout Christian, took him to the village Methodist Chapel, thinking that he might find help there. He accompanied her with great reluctance; he was thoroughly bored and the only thing that made any impression on him during the service was a quotation from the Book of Joel:

> *I will restore to you the years that the locust hath eaten.*

John felt that the words 'the years that the locust hath eaten' exactly described the wasted years of the war.

Although John did not go back to the church, on the morning of Sunday, 13 October 1946, he had the radio on and happened to hear a talk by the Bishop of Singapore, the Right Reverend J. Leonard Wilson. Like John, the Bishop had been a prisoner in Changi, although an internee in the civilian section. He, also, had been interrogated and cruelly tortured. What impressed John was the Bishop's total lack of bitterness. Unlike himself, Leonard Wilson had not only continued to believe in God, but had emerged from his ordeal with deepened faith.

Meanwhile, John returned to his pre-war job as a salesman, work he did with considerable success but with little real satisfaction. He had a succession of girl friends until, on 1 April 1947, he met Alyson. She seemed different from the other girls he had taken out. She was quiet and intelligent, the only thing he had against her at the time was that she was a practising Christian, although a very attractive one. In a strange way, John now seemed to be constantly confronted by people to whom God was real and important, and who were eager to share their beliefs.

John continued to make extensive enquiries concerning the fate of Marquita and Phiphine. At last he received the good news that they were alive and well. He took his parents and Alyson to Paris to meet Marquita. She told them how they had managed to survive, and said that she believed God had answered their prayers. John was sceptical, and was surprised by the vehemence with which she rebuked him, when she said with obvious conviction, 'Of course there *are* miracles and of course there *is* a God.'

Gradually, through this kind of encounter and particularly through the influence of Alyson and another young Christian, John Wadham, John Dodd came to see for himself that there *was* meaning to life, that there *was* a God of love, and that his own life had been spared for a purpose. One day, very simply but definitely, John surrendered his life to God. It was not a dramatic happening, he does not even remember what day it was, but it did produce a dramatic change in his life. In John's own words, 'It was like a Liverpool football fan becoming an Everton supporter.' Everything seemed changed and fresh, life became worthwhile once more.

John was now eager to do something that would be of service to God and to his fellow men and women. He joined the local Methodist Church at which he was now a regular worshipper. The minister, The Revd Tom Foinette, asked John if he would try to start a Sunday School in an old disused chapel in Havenstreet, a village near the centre of the Isle of Wight. Because of his drive and enthusiasm, John soon had a thriving Sunday School which he ran there with great success for the following ten years. His energy and capacity for work were boundless, and he also ran the Wootton Bridge Youth Club, accompanied Alyson to Bible study classes and joined the Christian Businessmen's Association. His new-found happiness was complete when, on 1 September 1951, he and Alyson were married.

Five months later, John was back in gaol—this time not as a prisoner, but as a *visitor*. Knowing something of John's experiences as a prisoner of war, Tom Foinette had asked him if he had ever considered prison visiting as a form of voluntary service. As a result, John began visiting at Parkhurst Prison on the Isle of Wight.

The experience affected him profoundly, not merely because he was sorry for those whom he visited, but also because *he knew how they felt*. The men themselves soon became aware of his unusual understanding and came to regard him as a welcome and trusted friend. John found that the men were usually eager to discuss religion and, after some months, four of them professed conversion. Although John knew that the real test of the genuineness of their new-found faith would come on their release from prison, he was thrilled to see the change in their lives; almost overnight they became happier and more confident, having gained a new self-respect.

John's mother also took a great interest in the prison and one day asked him,'Do you think any of your men would like it if I wrote to them sometimes?' Knowing that most recidivists receive very few, if any, letters, John encouraged her to make a start by writing to one or two of his own prison acquaintances. Her letters proved to be so welcome that before long she was writing some hundreds a year, and she became known throughout the British prison system as 'Mother Dodd'. At first, John thought that she might be put off if she discovered the nature of the crimes committed by some of her correspondents. However, she merely said, 'We don't know what sort of things *we* might have done if *we'd* been brought up in different homes, dear,' and carried on with her self-appointed task.

In recognition of the value of his work, John was appointed deputy to the visiting Methodist Chaplain at Parkhurst. He now led a weekly discussion group and sometimes preached in the prison chapel; he was in regular contact with about eighty men. From his growing knowledge of the prisoners he met, John came to believe that his mother might be correct in linking criminal behaviour with inadequate up-bringing. He also discovered that many men released from prison soon returned to a life of crime simply because they had nowhere to go, no job prospects and no-one to help them.

By 1956, John had two daughters, a new house and new employers. Still working as a salesman, and very successful at his job, he was earning a good income. He had also achieved some degree of status in the community and had the added pleasure of doing valuable voluntary work for an under-privileged section of society. Yet, despite all this, he was becoming restless again and dissatisfied with his job. More-over, his mind was increasingly occupied with the problem of what more could be done for the habitual criminal. 'They don't want to be criminals,' he explained to his wife, 'they are fail-ures. They fail at everything—especially crime. They've been crippled as surely as if they'd lost their legs . . . they need help.'

Unbeknown to John, a voluntary organisation of professional men and women, named *Christian Teamwork*, shared a similar concern. As an experiment, they were considering setting up a 'half-way house', a house where men coming out of prison could live until they had adjusted to ordinary life. The ex-prisoners selected would be expected to work and to pay a nominal rent, but they would live as a family with a Christian couple acting as 'house-parents'. The idea was sound, but they needed the right man to put it into effect. Oliver Stott, a member of Christian Teamwork, remembered meeting John Dodd two years prev-iously and knew something of his work in prison visiting.

As yet no house had been purchased, but in March 1958 Christian Teamwork invited John to become warden and house-father to a proposed 'family' of fifteen 'old lags'. It meant moving from the Isle of Wight and large drop in income, but to John it seemed as though Joel's prophecy was about to be ful-filled in his own life: 'I will restore unto you the years that the locust hath eaten. . . .' He now understood that those years of imprisonment in Changi had not been wasted, for he could have had no better preparation for the work he was about to undertake. Alyson, who had just given birth to their third daughter, agreed that he should accept the invitation, and they moved with Mother Dodd to the mainland, to a house at Compton, near Winchester.

The house Christian Teamwork hoped to acquire for the first half-way house was a farm called *Langley House*. They registered themselves as a charity under the name of *The Langley House Trust*, and managed to raise some money for the purchase. However, unknown to them, someone else made a higher offer, and Langley House was sold over their heads. They now had a Trust and a name for their proposed after-care organisation, but no house. Fortunately, they found an alternative, a dilapidated private hotel called Elderfield. It. was situated conveniently in Otterbourne, the next village to Compton— where the Dodd family were now living.

Early in the planning stage, it was decided that instead of acting as house-father, John should become the general secretary of the newly formed Langley House Trust. His job would include fund-raising, the selection of residents and overall administration. However, one of his first tasks was to scrounge furniture with which to equip the empty hotel. Next, a pleasant middle-aged couple, previously officers in the Salvation Army, were appointed as house-parents, and in June 1959, the first Langley House opened its doors to fifteen men, some of whom John had known in Parkhurst.

Nobody could foresee the difficulties involved in this pioneer work of rehabilitation. At first it was thought that if they selected professing Christians, provided them with a six-week stay in a family environment and obtained employment for them, then habitual criminals could be transformed into good citizens. It proved to be a vain hope. Elderfield's fifteen residents turned out to be a 'family' of clashing personalities who acted like jealous children, always seeking the attention of the house-parents and continually testing their friendship by demanding more and more of them. After three months, the first house-parents had to retire because of utter exhaustion.

The immediate question was: who would replace them? John

was already fully occupied raising money, speaking at meetings, visiting prisons, interviewing prospective residents and finding jobs for the men. Alyson, apart from looking after their own children, was already doing the Trust's clerical work. However, Mother Dodd came to the rescue by offering to look after Elderfield until new house-parents could be found. She was a great success. To the men she was all that a mother should be, and they responded to her immediately.

Typical of the residents who rallied round to support her was Scouse. A stocky man in his forties, he had spent a poverty-stricken childhood in a Liverpool slum. His father regularly returned home drunk and Scouse used to watch in terror as his father kicked his mother unconscious. Scouse himself grew up to be a burglar. Eventually, he was re-arrested; at his trial he asked for seventy-seven other burglaries to be taken into consideration. He was sentenced to ten years Preventive Detention. Scouse was one of the men converted to Christianity through John Dodd's visits to Parkhurst Prison.

At Elderfield, Scouse assumed the role of its full-time maintenance man. He worked hard and appeared to be settling down well. Ironically, trouble came from an attempt to help Scouse in his personal life. Both John and Scouse felt that if he could find the right kind of wife, he would be able to return to ordinary life. John arranged for Scouse to correspond through a Lonely Hearts Club. After many disappointments, he met Kitty, an attractive, sensible widow, and after a number of meetings the couple were engaged to be married. Unfortunately, Kitty's relatives intervened and persuaded her to break off the engagement. When she told Scouse, he was deeply hurt. That evening, he packed his bags, marched round to John's house and hurled abuse at him, saying, 'It's all *your* fault.' Then he ran away into the gathering darkness, leaving John saddened by a sense of failure.

The first Christmas at Elderfield was one never to be forgotten. The Dodd's decorated the house, bought presents for each resident and prepared a pre-Christmas dinner especially for the benefit of those who would be away on Christmas Day.

They were eating plum pudding when, without any warning—and without any apparent reason—one of the men leaped up and grabbed John by the throat. It seemed as if all the repressed tension of the previous weeks suddenly erupted. Four men hurled themselves on John and his assailant. Others began to fight among themselves. The table was overturned and the men struggled on the floor amid the remains of the dinner. The police were called, and John and Alyson opened the door to them still wearing party hats, but feeling in anything but a party mood.

At this stage the project seemed like a dismal failure and John might well have given up. However, not only was his conviction as strong as ever that God had guided him into this work, but once more his iron determination became evident. If the Japanese had been unable to make him give in, nor would anyone else. He reviewed the first six months of the project. The experiment had not been a total failure. For instance, he had noticed that although most of the residents had been thieves at some stage in their lives, at Elderfield there had been no stealing. Furthermore, most of the men had responded positively to the love and acceptance shown to them by the staff. What they needed was more time, certainly much longer than the six weeks originally thought to be sufficient for their rehabilitation.

John began again. New house-parents were appointed. The selection of residents became more discriminating, for experience showed that Langley House had not yet acquired the resources to cope with men who were seriously disturbed mentally or those who had a history of violence. On the other hand, from 1960 onwards, the Trust was prepared to accept both Christians and *non*-Christians alike. John had become convinced that the main criterion of selection should be whether a man needed help and whether Langley House was likely to be able to help him.

January 1961 marked the beginning of the expansion of the work of the Trust. John received a letter which simply said, 'I have recently read an article about the work of the Langley

House Trust and I am interested in buying you another house in Yorkshire.' The lady who had written purchased for the Trust a large old house called Box Tree Cottage, it was situated in a pleasant residential area of Bradford.

The new Home was opened in June 1961. One of its first residents was Braddy, a twenty-one year old epileptic with a bad stammer, a young man who was totally lacking in self-confidence. His mother was a prostitute and he had spent most of his childhood waiting out in the street, summer and winter, while she entertained her clients. He had committed a series of minor offences so inexpertly that it was obvious that he was seeking a prison sentence; for Braddy, life inside prison was much less threatening than life outside. He could hardly believe his good fortune when he came to live at Box Tree Cottage and found that not only was he provided with good meals and a clean bed, but also, for the first time in his life, there were those who really *cared* about him. Responding to the love shown to him by the House Parents, Braddy offered to help in the kitchen. The house-mother noticed that he had a natural aptitude for cooking and she taught him all she knew. The more proficient he became the less he stammered and the more his confidence grew. When he left Box Tree Cottage a year later he went as under-chef at a local hotel and after a time became the chief chef in a large hotel in Blackpool.

In spite of the many problems encountered during the first two and a half years of the Langley House project, the results were beginning to look promising. One hundred and ten discharged prisoners had been in residence for varying lengths of time. Of the seventy-five with whom John kept in touch, only nineteen received further prison sentences during the high-risk period following their release. In comparison, Home Office figures covering the same period showed that of those who returned *direct* from detention to ordinary life, fifty per cent had been reconvicted within three years; it was significant that the majority were reconvicted within the first year of their release.

Although these figures were encouraging, John had come to see that the real results of the work of Langley House were not to be assessed statistically. Apparent failure initially could turn to success in the long-term. For example, the man who had attacked John during the Christmas dinner at Elderfield arrived unexpectedly at the Dodds' house five years later and without any preamble simply said, 'Just thought I'd come and say thanks for all you did for me.'

Scouse, the former burglar, who had left Elderfield with such bitterness after failing to find a wife, had also been a disappointment to John at the time. However, he had returned to Liverpool and obtained a job in industry. Despite many obstacles, he made a determined effort to keep out of further trouble. He succeeded and he has been 'going straight' for nearly twenty years. From time to time he calls to see the Dodd family and reports on his progress. When he first came to Elderfield in 1959, his Prison Governor had written on his discharge report, 'He has not had any year free from imprisonment since 1934. I doubt if he can overcome that handicap. . . .' Now officially retired, Scouse has been invited to live permanently at one of the Langley House communities where his sense of humour, his understanding of former prisoners and his Christian experience would be invaluable.

But apparent *success* can also turn to unforeseen disaster. This was true of Percy, who came to Elderfield in 1960. In spite of a long record of petty larceny, he proved to be a trustworthy, model resident. Everyone was delighted when he married and settled down happily in a cottage nearby. Inexplicably, three months after the wedding, he killed his wife. Everyone connected with Langley House was deeply shocked. At his trial, an eminent brain specialist testified that Percy was subject to fits during which he was no longer responsible for his actions. A verdict was returned of: 'Not guilty of murder, but guilty of manslaughter on the ground of diminished responsibility.' Percy was sent first to Dartmoor and then to Parkhurst. Each summer John and family visit him there, and in between these visits he exchanges letters regularly with Mother Dodd and with Diana, one of John's three daughters.

In the early stages of the development of Langley House, one of John's most difficult tasks was to raise money for the Trust. This was mainly due to lack of sympathy in the general public for men who had been in prison. He was greatly helped, however, by *The Friends of Langley House*, a support organisation established at the commencement of the Trust in 1959 to assist in fund-raising and, equally important to John and his staff, to pray for their work.

For his part, John found it best to concentrate particularly on personal contacts for financial support. Through his friendship with the late Revd Dr Leslie Davison, then General Secretary of the Methodist Home Mission Department, the Methodist Church became one of the Trust's most generous supporters. It purchased Elderfield outright in December 1961, thereby relieving Langley House of its four hundred pounds annual lease. It also bought The Chalet, a pleasant house in a quiet street in Reading, which opened in August 1962.

Soon afterwards, the Cheltenham Council of Churches offered to provide a house in the Spa. For the first time John met with considerable opposition from some of the local residents. Eventually, a house named The Knole, was found in another part of the town, which opened its doors to the first residents in November 1963.

The opposition in Cheltenham showed John that there was an urgent need to change the public's attitude towards discharged prisoners. A friend at the BBC arranged for him to tell his story on the Radio series 'People Today'. The broadcast on 3 November 1963 made a profound impact. Money and offers to help poured in. There was one gift of a thousand pounds; another was for fifty and it was accompanied by a note which read, 'This is for you and your dear family and is *not* to be used on those dreadful men.' Although the well-meaning donor had completely missed the point of John's broadcast, most people who heard him began to think of the ex-prisoner in an entirely new light.

While working on his script for the broadcast, John was taken to Wormwood Scrubs Prison by Geoffrey Howard, the producer of the programme. On their arrival, there was a sudden, surprising glare of powerful lights. A broad-shouldered man stepped forward holding a microphone and said, 'Tonight, John Dodd, *This Is Your Life.*' Eamonn Andrews, the compère of this popular television programme, described his guest as, 'John Dodd, *man of courage and compassion*'. The programme, seen by an estimated ten million viewers, proved to be another very useful piece of publicity for his work.

A morale-boosting sign of official recognition and a new source of practical help came in 1966, when the Home Office made the first of its annual grants to the Langley House Trust. As a result, closer links were established with the Probation and After-Care Services. With the additional financial support, the Trust was able to fill some gaps in its programme of re-habilitation. For example, on the initiative of the Coventry Council of Churches, a house was specially designed and built to provide accommodation exclusively for *young* offenders. Further financial assistance came as a result of a public appeal and from a grant made by the City Council. It was named Murray Lodge and was opened by the Home Secretary in 1967.

Since its foundation, the members of the Trust had been concerned that frequently they had to turn away those who were *grossly* inadequate. Yet, it was men such as these, men who could not cope with even the most ordinary demands of life, who were the very ones who most needed help. John and his co-workers nursed a hope of creating sheltered communities where the residents could stay for an unspecified length of time, doing something useful within their own capacities, and learning to come to terms with themselves. In 1969, their hope was fulfilled when the Home Mission Department of the Methodist Church bought Wing Grange at Oakham in Rutland and leased it to Langley House, rent free. There the men can work either in the art and craft workshops, in the gardens or on the farm. What is produced they either use themselves or sell to the public from their own shop.

Since the commencement of the Langley House project in 1959, nearly six thousand men have passed through its Homes. Starting with just one Half-way House, the Trust now sponsors a complex of a dozen interdependent homes offering varying levels of support for about two hundred and forty men at any one time. There are now four Half-way Houses, five Therapeutic Sheltered Communities, and three Retirement Sheltered Communities. The latter are for men of, or approaching, retirement age who have no employment prospects but who, nonetheless, are able to make themselves useful in the house and gardens of the Community.

As General Secretary, John is responsible for raising at least thirty thousand pounds a year from voluntary sources to meet the ever-increasing running costs of the Trust. He has two assistant general secretaries, one of whom is responsible for the selection of all the residents. All three visit the Houses regularly and act both as a link between the various houses and as a support to the House Parents. Each House has its own Advisory Group and a Liaison Probation Officer who is the link between the House and the statutory authority. Further plans for the future are always under consideration and John reports that such plans 'concern particularly ways in which we can help the types of men who, for different reasons, we are unable to have at our existing houses, mostly because they require more individual attention than we can provide'.

Even though after-care for the discharged prisoner has improved on a national scale in recent years and other hostels have been opened in Britain, Langley House is unique in that it is a specifically *Christian* organisation. Although the Houses are not used for indoctrination, the devoted service of the members of staff is a witness in itself to a faith which is essentially expressed in action.

John has travelled widely, visiting other countries to see the way in which similar organisations are seeking to help discharged prisoners. In addition, he has been a member of the After-Care and Parole Committee of the Advisory Council on Probation and After-Care to the Home Office. This was an appointment which enabled him to share the many lessons he had learned from practical experience and it also gave him an opportunity to share in the shaping of official policy nationally.

The significance of John Dodd's work is not limited to the organisation he has built up. Equally, it lies in the part he has played in helping to change the public's attitude towards criminals. He has demonstrated the importance of differentiating between the cold, calculating crime-for-profit criminal and those for whom Langley House particularly caters, that is, the inadequates and social misfits, many of whom have had a deprived childhood. In this process of enlightenment, he has given evidence to Government Committees, interviews to the Press, television and radio, and spoken to a variety of audiences including Rotary Clubs, Round Tables, church groups and schools.

In spite of his extremely busy life and the extensive travelling involved in his work, John is essentially a family man. His home is still at Combpyne in Compton, which is also the headquarters of the Trust. Alyson, his wife, continues to be actively associated with the running of the Trust. One of their daughters has married a young man who came to work with Langley House as a Community Service Volunteer. Mother Dodd, too, over ninety years old at the time of writing, still supports the work through prayer.

In the Queen's Birthday Honours List of 1968, John Dodd was awarded the M.B.E. His work, and that of Langley House as a whole, received further recognition when, on 16 November 1973, H.R.H. Princess Alexandra made an official visit to Forncett Grange, the Trust's Sheltered Community near Norwich.

John belongs to Chandler's Ford Methodist Church. His minister, the Revd John S. Stephens, describes him as 'truly humble for one who has achieved so much. He is a very sincere evangelical Christian. The sincerity of John's experience dominates all he does, and therefore he is impatient with the trivia of Church life, but wonderfully patient with those who are most in need of the Christian gospel. Every aspect of his work reflects his Christian discipleship.'

John Dodd stepped out on the path to discipleship when, unintentionally, he heard Bishop Leonard Wilson's radio broadcast at the end of World War II. It is significant that in that memorable broadcast, the Bishop said of those who had tortured him, 'I saw them, not as they were, not as they had been, but as they were capable of becoming, redeemed by the power of Christ. . . .'[1] This is precisely the way in which John regards the men who come to Langley House.

John's work has been described by Dr Horace King, P.C., a former Speaker of the House of Commons, as 'one of the noblest social endeavours being undertaken today'.[2] The Revd Dr Leslie Davison, who, as Secretary of the Methodist Home Mission Department, had a particular interest in the development of Langley House, sums up John Dodd's place in contemporary social history:

> 'Time and again in the history of humanity our whole attitude to a social problem is changed because a man comes along with a concern. He has to be a particular kind of man, with enormous resilience, courage and persistence. He must know his subject from the inside. He must know how to enlist the aid of others whose experience and skills go beyond his own. He makes faster progress if he charms people and makes friends quickly. But above all, he must be able to communicate his own compassion and concern and help other people to feel as he feels and to see the issues for what they are. John Dodd is such a man. . . .'[3]

Langley House as at August 1977:

Half-Way Houses:

Coventry	Murray Lodge (For Teenagers)
Bradford	Box Tree Cottage
Poole	Langdon House
Reading	The Chalet

Therapeutic Sheltered Communities:

Buckminster	(Grantham) Hanby House
Norwich	Forncett Grange
Otterbourne	(Winchester) Elderfield
Wing	(Oakham) Wing Grange
Taunton	House of St. Martin

Retirement Sheltered Communities:

Cheltenham	The Knole
Lancaster	Longcroft
Rochester	The Shrubbery

References

Grateful acknowledgement is made to the Authors and Publishers of the literature cited below:

1. 'John Leonard Wilson—Confessor of the Faith': Roy McKay: Hodder and Stoughton Ltd, 1974, p. 34

2. Address given at the 10th Annual Open Day at Elderfield, 1969: quoted in the Langley House Newsletter No. 29

3. 'Road from Singapore': Diana Norman: Hodder and Stoughton Ltd, 1973, p. 7

For Further Reading

'Road from Singapore': Diana Norman: Hodder and Stoughton Ltd, 1970; Pbk. Ed. 1973

'Prisoner of the Jungle—John Dodd'· Diana Norman: Biography for Today Series: Lutterworth Educational, 1972

'Miracle of the River Kwai': Ernest Gordon: Fontana, 1963

'John Leonard Wilson—Confessor of the Faith': Roy McKay: Hodder and Stoughton Ltd, 1973; Pbk. Ed. 1974

Other similar stories: see under chap. 7—Ernest Gordon

On Other Work for Prisoners

'Forgotten Men—Common Lodging Houses': Merfyn Turner: National Council of Social Security, 1960

'A Pretty Sort of Prison': Merfyn Turner: Pall Mall, 1964

'Prisoners' Progress': Merfyn Turner: Housemans Press, 1968

'The Unknown Citizen': Tony Parker: Penguin, 1966

Films

Although no films are available specifically on the work of Langley House, there are a number of films on similar aspects of work for prisoners. They are available from Concord Films Council Ltd, Nacton, Ipswich, Suffolk, IP10 0JZ. The following are a selection:

'After Prison, What? The work of the John Howard Society': Nat. Film Board of Canada: B/W. 11 mins.

'Golborne—One Man's Answer': the Revd Bertram Peake and the Golborne Centre, London (see chap. 12, Sally Trench). B/W. 30 mins.

'People Like Albert': the work of the National Association for the Care and Resettlement of Offenders: 1973: Col. 30 mins.

'Seymour': a man comes out of prison with only a few pence in his pocket: Granada 'World in Action', 1973: Col. 30 mins.

'Prison: The Alternatives: experiments in rehabilitation': BBC 'Man Alive', 1974: B/W. 45 mins.

'Tougher than Punishment': Peper Harow, an approved school which now operates as a therapeutic community: BBC 'Man Alive', 1974: B/W. 50 mins.

For Further Information

The General Secretary: Langley House, 'Combpyne', Tilden Road, Compton, Winchester, SO21 2DQ, Hampshire

Langley House publishes a 'Newsletter' obtainable from the address above

CHAPTER FIVE

The Pathfinder

Leonard Cheshire VC DSO DFC

Born 1917

On 13 November 1946, at Buckingham Palace, a young Wing-Commander stood before King George VI to receive the Victoria Cross—the highest decoration for valour given in the British Commonwealth. On this occasion the award was not for one particular act of gallantry, but for four years of sustained courage shown during a hundred bomber raids. Part of the citation read:

> *He led his squadron personally on every occasion, always undertaking the most dangerous and difficult task of marking the target alone from a low level in the face of strong defences. In June 1944, when marking the target at Le Havre in broad daylight and without cloud cover, he dived well below the range of the light batteries before releasing his marker bombs and came very near to being destroyed by the strong barrage. Wing Commander Cheshire's cold and calculated acceptance of risks is exemplified by his conduct in an attack on Munich in April 1944. . . . In four years of fighting against the bitterest opposition he has maintained a record of outstanding personal achievement, placing himself invariably at the forefront of the battle. What he did in the Munich operation was typical of the careful planning, brilliant execution and contempt for danger which has established for Wing Commander Cheshire a reputation second to none in Bomber Command.*

Leonard Cheshire was also awarded the Distinguished Service Order with two additional bars, and the Distinguished Flying Cross, thereby becoming one of the most highly decorated airmen of the Second World War.

Leonard Cheshire was born in Chester on 7 September 1917. Two years later his family moved to Oxford where Leonard spent most of his childhood. At the age of fourteen he obtained a scholarship from the Dragon School at Oxford to enter the Public School at Stowe. The headmaster of Stowe recalls that, 'He was very successful as a schoolboy in the ordinary sense.' At this stage in his life, however, he gave no indication of the distinction he was to achieve by the time he was twenty-six.

In 1936, Cheshire became an undergraduate at Merton College, Oxford. Like many of his contemporaries he was a rebel against convention, defying University rules and taking a particular delight in spectacular escapades. He enjoyed drinking in taverns that were out of bounds, he gambled at dog-racing tracks and made regular (unauthorised) visits to the night clubs of the West End of London. These trips were made possible by the acquisition of a second-hand Alfa-Romeo sports car. The problem of gaining admission to the locked College on his return did not present insuperable difficulties. He had a gift for getting on well with people from all social backgrounds and was soon on very good terms with Fred, the stoker of Merton's boilers. Many a time, in the early hours of the morning, Cheshire crawled through the coal hole, conveniently left open by the obliging stoker. These nocturnal adventures meant that Bert, his college servant, sometimes had the utmost difficulty in arousing him for morning roll call. The only alternative to answering roll call was attendance at morning prayers, and Cheshire regarded roll call as the lesser of two evils. 'Mr Cheshire never once darkened the door of the chapel,' Bert recalls. 'He told me prayers didn't agree with him.'

The bright red sports car was an expression of its owner's flamboyant way of life. On one occasion he persuaded a friend to accompany him on a return visit to his old school at Stowe.

After having tea with the headmaster, Cheshire drove off, eager to make an impression on an admiring group of school boy spectators. The car roared down the narrow, curving, gravel drive. On the bend it went out of control, hurtled off the drive, crashed through a sight-screen on the boundary of the school cricket field and came to rest on the pitch, where a match was in progress.

Cheshire joined the University Air Squadron soon after starting at Oxford but for several months remained a non-flying and inactive member. Eventually he decided to take instruction and was assigned to Flight Lieutenant C. Whitworth. The flying-instructor was irritated by his new pupil's cocky manner and, on their first flight, went through a series of manoeuvres which would have made the average beginner too sick to continue. Cheshire, however, simply asked for more, and Whitworth realised that, despite his brashness, this young student was a born flyer. Looking back, Whitworth says, 'I was sure in Cheshire's case, after three or four lessons, that he had all the makings of an exceptionally daring pilot.'[1] He flew solo for the first time on 8 June 1937 and, in the Autumn, he joined the RAF Volunteer Reserve.

When war came in 1939, Cheshire, now twenty-one, waited impatiently for his call-up papers. He says of himself at that time, 'I was a peculiar mixture of moral and immoral, and the war came at a lucky moment to divert my ambitions, energy and queer ideals into legalised channels of excitement.'[2] He was called up into the RAF and sent for training as a bomber pilot. He applied himself to the course with such enthusiasm and self-confidence that the chief flying instructor said of him, 'This chap's a phenomenon. I swear he'll either kill himself soon or become a very famous pilot.'[3]

His first operational unit was 102 Squadron, based at Driffield, Yorkshire. On 9 June 1940, newly commissioned, Pilot-Officer Cheshire took off in a Whitley aircraft on his first bombing mission; the target was an important bridge at Abberville in France. He took part in several more attacks on targets in France followed by raids on the industrial and armament cities of Germany interspersed with submarine spotting patrols over the Atlantic. It was on a raid on Cologne that he won his first citation. They were flying over the city preparing to release their bombs, when, suddenly, there was a blinding flash and a shattering explosion. Another flash and the bomber shuddered, lurched and began plunging down. Half dazed, with shells still exploding all round the aircraft, Cheshire wrestled with the controls until at last the engines responded and the plane levelled out. The plastic dome of the cockpit was smashed, a large section of the fuselage torn away and the petrol tank on fire. Although injured, the crew managed to extinguish the fire before it spread further. In spite of their grave predicament, Cheshire decided to drop their bombs on the target as planned. Only when the last bomb had fallen on the network of railway lines below did he turn the Whitley homewards. Their young wireless operator, who was on his first flight, was very badly burned; the radio and most of the instruments were shattered, the maps burned. Nonetheless, Cheshire nursed the bomber back to England, making a perfect landing. Two days later he learned that he had been awarded the D.S.O.

Cheshire was later posted to No. 35 Halifax Squadron, but while these new aircraft were undergoing modifications, he was sent to the USA on special duties. Here he met Constance Binney, who later became his wife (unfortunately, this marriage to a woman considerably older than himself was not a success, and they were divorced before the end of the war). On his return to England, Cheshire flew with his Squadron on raid after raid. At the completion of his first tour of duty, when he had flown on about fifty missions, he was awarded the D.F.C. The citation referred to his *exceptional keenness, initiative and devotion to duty*, and to his *important role in building up crews*. It stated that his success had been *largely due to his personal standards* which had been an example for others to follow. This new award added to Cheshire's growing reputation among the general public. He was now regularly featured in the popular press as a national hero. His exploits became yet more widely known when he wrote a book entitled *Bomber Pilot*, from which extracts appeared under sensational headlines in a Sunday newspaper.

In September 1942, Cheshire was made a Wing Commander and posted to 76 Squadron. Here he displayed his flair for getting on well with all ranks. In particular his ground crews were devoted to him. As one aircraft fitter put it, 'It was nice to feel all the time that we had a human being for a boss, someone who appreciated our work and wasn't too stand-offish to come and tell us so . . . I don't think I've ever worked harder in my life than I worked for Cheshire.' In April 1943, he was promoted to the rank of Group Captain and posted to Marston Moor to supervise the re-training of bomber crews. The following July he was back again at Buckingham Palace, this time to receive a bar to his D.S.O.

Cheshire soon grew weary of administrative work and longed for operational flying again. He voluntarily dropped rank in order that he might succeed Guy Gibson as Commander of the famous 617 squadron, known as the 'Dambusters'. It was with this élite squadron that Cheshire developed a low-level marking technique which enabled heavy bombs to be dropped with great accuracy on specially selected targets, such as the launching sites for the German V2* rockets. A British scientist, Barnes Wallis, had developed an enormously powerful bomb capable of penetrating the tons of concrete used to protect these new weapons. The bomb (known as a Tallboy) had to be dropped precisely *alongside* the concrete fortifications in order to explode beneath their foundations. Cheshire led the first attack in a Mosquito.† Flying in at tree-top level, he identified the target and dropped marker bombs. The bomb-aimers in the eighteen Lancasters flying high overhead then used the smoking

---

* V2: a rocket-propelled projectile with which Hitler planned to annihilate London and force Britain to surrender. The projectile carrying tons of explosive was capable of rising very high before descending silently on its target.

† Mosquito: a fast, manoeuvrable British fighter-bomber. In later raids, Cheshire used the single-seater American Mustang in which he had to act as his own pilot, navigator, wireless operator and bomb-aimer.

markers as their target and dropped their bombs with devastating effect. There is little doubt that the success of this and other similar raids prevented the destruction of London by the deadly V2 rockets.

Cheshire personally led 617 Squadron on some forty pin-pointing, low-level attacks on bomb dumps, rocket and aero-factories, bridges and railway tunnels, in France and Germany. He was awarded a second bar to his D.S.O. in recognition of his *magnificent achievements* over France. One of his most daring missions was a daylight raid on the E-boat pens at Le Havre, when fifty-three boats were destroyed. For this raid, and for the courage shown in the hundred operations he had now completed, he was awarded the British Commonwealth's supreme award for valour, the Victoria Cross. Cheshire, however, felt that the award had been given as much to the men he led, as to himself.

For four years Cheshire faced constant danger and fatigue, surviving against all odds. In spite of his protests, he was now ordered to rest from flying. He was sent to India as a Staff officer and later went to Washington as a member of the British Joint Staff Mission. Ironically, it was in an American aircraft and travelling only as a passenger, that he flew on his last operational flight. It was 9 August 1945, the eve of the end of the war; the occasion was the dropping of the second atomic bomb, and he and the scientist, Dr William Penny, went as official British observers. The B-29 they were flying in became separated from the aircraft carrying the bomb. Suddenly, when they were still forty miles from their target —the Japanese city of Nagasaki—they saw a blinding, white flash which was followed by an explosion which caused their aircraft to rock violently. A ball of fire shot upwards and then an enormous mushroom-shaped cloud of smoke rose slowly into the sky. Within a few seconds Nagasaki was virtually obliterated. That scene of sickening horror would always remain in Cheshire's memory.

He left the RAF in 1946 and spent the next few months trying to find something worthwhile to do. He lectured, wrote articles and even ran a flower-delivery service. Acutely aware of the appalling potentialities of the atomic bomb, he campaigned for the outlawing of war. He also understood the difficulties that so many ex-servicemen were experiencing as they tried to re-adjust to civilian life, and he became their unofficial champion. He was conscious of a growing desire to do something practical for them and eventually hit upon the idea of a co-operative community for ex-service people. The project was designated V.I.P.*—Vade in Pace—and was operated from Gumley Hall, a large house and gardens near Market Harborough, which Cheshire had been offered rent-free for twelve months. His plan was to create a colony of fellow-idealists who would support themselves by market gardening, rearing dogs, rabbits and mice, and by making toys and household woodware.

It was during this period of his life that he began to take an interest in religion. Some months previously, in a fashionable London night club, he had become involved in a discussion about the origin and destiny of mankind. At that time, Cheshire had little sympathy with religion and declared that it was absurd to believe that God existed, except as a figure of speech and a convenient way of explaining the voice of conscience. An attractive young woman unexpectedly intervened, accusing him of talking nonsense. 'Of course there is a God', she said, 'and he is a *real* person, not a figure of speech.' At the time, the incident appeared to have made little impression on him, but later Cheshire recognised that it was one of the landmarks in his search for faith. By the time he moved in at Gumley Hall, he had come to realise that a religion which taught men to love their enemies might be more successful than science in removing the causes of war. In spite of his previous indifference, he began to go occasionally to Church.

Although Cheshire's enthusiasm was limitless, the Gumley Hall project was a failure and many of the 'colonists' became disillusioned and left. Undefeated, he decided to try again else-where. In 1947, accompanied by a loyal remnant of the original

*The initials V.I.P. always stood for Vade In Pace—'Go in Peace', not 'Very Important Persons'.

V.I.Ps, he moved to Le Court, a large house near Liss, in Hampshire. A syndicate of city businessmen had been persuaded to put up the money for its purchase. They hoped that it might be possible to run a profitable soft fruit farm and market garden on the large estate purchased with the house.

However, the physical and mental strain involved in establishing the V.I.P. Association proved too much for Cheshire's health and he was persuaded to take six months rest. He went to Canada and stayed with a retired Bishop, an old friend of his father and mother. Here, amidst the majestic pine-forests of British Columbia, he became convinced, not only of God's existence, but also of his living presence. He began to pray, spontaneously, as a natural response to the Creator of so much splendour and beauty.

At the end of November, Cheshire received an urgent cable: 'Return as soon as possible. V.I.P. in serious trouble.' He returned to find the project bankrupt and the residents at loggerheads. Within five months of his return, only two of the original colonists remained. There seemed nothing to be done except admit failure and sell Le Court. It was then that he was told about a former member of the colony, Arthur Dykes, an elderly man suffering from incurable cancer. He was occupying a much-needed hospital bed and authorities asked Cheshire to find somewhere else for him. This proved impossible, and Cheshire decided to take him 'home' to Le Court, where he nursed him with great care and affection. Dykes was a Christian, a devout Roman Catholic. They often discussed religion and Cheshire was immensely impressed by his cheerful courage despite the pain he was suffering. Dykes knew that he had not long to live; nevertheless, his faith remained unshaken and he died with dignity and serenity.

Although Cheshire regarded himself as an Anglican, he felt increasingly drawn towards Roman Catholicism and he requested instruction by the priest who had visited Dykes during his illness. After some months of instruction during which he read, thought, and also discussed religion with clergy of other denominations, Cheshire gradually came to a decision. As a result, on 23 December 1948, he was formally received into the Roman Catholic Church.

Before Arthur Dykes had died, Cheshire had taken in another patient, a ninety-three year old woman who was bedridden, deaf and senile. By Christmas 1949, he had thirty-two patients and a growing number of staff. He felt convinced that he had at last stumbled upon—or been led to—his true vocation. He took in anyone who came to the door—the old and helpless, the physically and mentally handicapped, those who had been in jail; anyone, in fact, who had nowhere else to go. They were admitted irrespective of race, creed or social status. His over-riding concern was to provide them with a home which was as much theirs as it was his, and to restore their dignity and self-respect. A former hospital almoner who joined his staff commented on the 'the air of almost unbroken tranquillity' which pervaded the home. Of Cheshire, she says, 'His greatest gift was undoubtedly the consolation he brought to the dying. He would never leave them, night or day until they had stopped breathing; he hardly bothered to eat or sleep, and every one of the seven or eight men and women who died that summer seemed to die happily and without fear.'[4] Cheshire grew to trust God in everything, including money matters. When asked how he hoped to finance the home, he simply replied, 'Don't worry. God will provide.'

Eventually, the long hours, the endless responsibility and the constant demands on his good nature and patience proved too great a strain. Once again he had worked himself to the point of break-down. He was persuaded to leave Le Court in the care of a body of trustees while he found a less exacting job. Early in 1951, he was taken on the staff of Vickers-Armstrong (manufacturers of aircraft and defensive weapons). He went to live at Tredannack in Cornwall, near the half-disused airfield which was to be his base. He had been allocated a Spitfire for his own use but although he enjoyed being in the air again, his thoughts often turned to Le Court, and the needs of the suffering. One day, flying over the airfield, he noticed some derelict Nissen huts not far from the cottage where he was living. At once he saw the possibility of using one of them for a second home for the sick and disabled. He enlisted the help of service personnel and civilians, and together they repaired and re-decorated one of the abandoned huts. They laid on water and electric light and equipped it with beds, cooker and furniture—all donated by local well-wishers. The converted hut was named St Teresa's and the new home's first patient was admitted on 11 May 1950.

In March 1952, Cheshire made the break with Vickers-Armstrong and set about the restoration of another hut on the same airfield. This was transformed into a third home and was named Holy Cross. Towards the end of August, however, Cheshire was himself admitted to hospital suffering from tuberculosis of the lung. His condition was so serious that he had to undergo four extensive chest operations and spent the next two years in either hospital or sanatorium.

Far from being inactive, he used the days spent in bed to think, plan, dictate letters and conduct interviews. Several important new projects were launched from his sick-room. Three weeks before he had been admitted to hospital, Cheshire had decided to tour the country preaching a simple and practical version of the Christian Faith. As he lay incapacitated, he had the idea of buying buses and using them for a 'crusade on wheels'. Accordingly, a second-hand bus was purchased and a volunteer recruited to drive it to various sites in London. The bus was furnished with a tableau-display and equipped to broadcast a selection of talks which Cheshire recorded in hospital. The idea proved successful and a second bus was purchased; the two buses were then used to tour England, visiting most of the large cities and drawing a crowd wherever they went. One of the tableaux which Cheshire designed featured the Holy Shroud*. It aroused considerable public interest, so much so that Cheshire, who was convinced of its authenticity, wrote two widely read articles and a booklet

---

*The Holy Shroud: a narrow piece of linen cloth alleged to be the burial sheet of Christ. It is claimed to be impressed with the image of Christ's face and the stains on it are said to be the imprints of Christ's wounds.

outlining the story behind the discovery and subsequent investigation of the Shroud. Another scheme launched while he was convalescing, was the organisation of air charter trips to Lourdes.* Cheshire himself visited Lourdes on the first week-end he spent out of the Sanatorium, even though he still had a drainage tube in his chest. He received no miraculous cure, but came back spiritually refreshened.

While in hospital he also supervised the purchase and foundation of his fourth home, St Cecilia's, which was established in Bromley for the aged and incurably sick. Meanwhile, the old Le Court had been demolished and rebuilt as a home specialising in the care of young people who were chronically sick and disabled.

With time to reflect on what he might do when his treatment was completed, Cheshire considered the possibility of entering the priesthood or becoming a member of a closed order of monks. However, by the time he left the Sanatorium, he had come to the conclusion that his mission would always be the relief of the incurably sick, handicapped and needy. He also concluded that he could best help such people, not by nursing them himself, nor by direct involvement in the day to day management of the homes, but by *founding* new homes wherever there was an area of need. As in the case of the four homes already established, he could then put the management of each new home in the hands of a committee, chosen to be as representative as possible of the local community. In order that there should be some body with overall responsibility he formed a central trust known as 'The Cheshire Foundation Homes for the Sick'. This Trust, which is a registered charity, presides over the homes, owns all the property and acts as a guarantor to the public that the individual homes are properly managed and in conformity with the general aims of the Cheshire Homes.†

*Lourdes: pilgrimage town in S.W. France possessing what are said to be 'healing waters'. It is also claimed that the Virgin Mary has appeared there, offering spiritual consolation.

† See end of chapter.

The time was now ripe for an extension of his work on an international scale. The initial impetus came when he received an invitation to go to India to advise on the possibility of commencing some kind of home or centre in Bombay. Cheshire went out to assess the situation and, with characteristic impetuosity, took over a small disused asbestos hut in a remote part of the jungle, away from the city. It was without light, water or sanitation. Nevertheless, Cheshire immediately installed four patients, and then set about the task of recruiting volunteers and begging materials to build two more huts. An Indian Trust was founded and since then, in response to the enthusiasm of various religious and official organisations, seventeen homes have been established in India.

Cheshire's influence overseas has not been limited to India. There are now over seventy Homes in more than thirty countries overseas, many more in the course of preparation. In Canada, for instance, six Homes have been opened within four years, and seven more are being planned. An interesting experiment is taking place in Papua New Guinea where there is a children's Home. The local community do not want the children to go on to a Home for adults, so as many as possible are being rehabilitated back into village life. Their parents and families are taught how to cope with those who are handicapped and when the young people return to their own homes, advice, help and support are provided by the Cheshire Home. Thus the Cheshire concept is adapted to meet particular needs in different countries so that, apart from Homes for the disabled and handicapped, there are Homes for destitute men and women, for 'burnt out' leprosy cases and for many other forms of human suffering. The Homes are all autonomous, raising their own funds locally and deciding their own policy.

There are nearly seventy Cheshire Homes in the United Kingdom. Two of these are for mentally handicapped children, and there are four hostels for the psychiatric rehabilitation of adults. All the Homes offer, not merely shelter, but an opportunity for the residents to use their skills to the full, both for their own satisfaction and in service to the local community.

In recent years many disabled people have wanted to marry, but were unable to do so because of the lack of suitable accommodation with the necessary care and support required. The Cheshire Foundation has tried to help these couples by providing flatlets, double rooms or bedsitters. For families with a disabled member, some Homes have provided bungalows and housing. The Foundation is at present pioneering a scheme to give domiciliary care to severely handicapped people in the community during the hours when the statutory District Nurse and Home Help Service is not available.

A new venture, the Cheshire Foundation Housing Association was formed in July 1976, and the first housing complex is to be built in Bournemouth. This will consist of eighty-four housing units alongside a small residential Cheshire home. The Home will provide a care and support service which will enable disabled people to be able to continue to live with parents or relatives who would not be able to cope without assistance.

On 22 July 1976, the name of the Foundation was changed to 'The Leonard Cheshire Foundation.' Many residents in Cheshire Homes did not like the description 'Homes for the *Sick*'. Leonard Cheshire himself felt that the term *'Home'* should be dropped as he believes that one of the future aims of the Foundation might be to fill a gap in the statutory Social Services by providing special care for disabled people living alone in their *own* houses.

Cheshire's work brought him into contact with Miss Sue Ryder. She has devoted her life to helping those victims of the Second World War who, as a result of their suffering in concentration camps and prisons, are now sick, homeless or in some kind of need. The Sue Ryder Foundation, besides building and renovating Homes and Hospitals for the sick and disabled of all ages in various countries of the world, also does social work and individual case work, operates mobile teams and provides medical care and equipment. Sue Ryder herself visits prisoners in Central and Eastern Europe held in over twenty prisons. Through a Holiday Scheme 4,000 survivors of the wartime

Resistance Movement and the concentration camps, their children and other disabled youngsters have been able to enjoy a holiday. From the start of her self-appointed mission of caring in 1945, Sue Ryder's work has been based on faith and carried out with the minimum of expense and administration. Money is raised by her Support Groups, who use various means of fund-raising including the well-known Sue Ryder Shops. Sue receives no salary and pays her own travelling expenses; she usually drives herself and reckons to cover over 50,000 miles a year. In 1957, in recognition of her outstanding humanitarian work, she was awarded the Order of the British Empire. She has also been honoured by the Governments of Poland and Yugoslavia and she is an Honorary Doctor of Laws of the University of Liverpool.

Leonard Cheshire and Sue Ryder first met in Poland and they were married in 1959. Their original proposal to link the Cheshire and Ryder Foundations did not prove practical, so the two organisations have remained legally separate, though working together as closely as possible. Out of their combined work there has evolved the Mission for the Relief of Suffering, an association of relief-work agencies having the same ideals and principles. The member organisations have pooled some of their resources and expertise in order to meet specific and urgent needs outside their own respective terms of reference. An example of this joint enterprise is the Ryder-Cheshire International Centre in Dehra Dun in North India. The Missionaries of Charity founded by Mother Teresa is also part of the Mission for the Relief of Suffering.

On 18 April 1975, Variety Clubs International, the world children's charity organisation, made a joint presentation to Cheshire and Sue Ryder of the Variety Clubs Humanitarian Award for 1974, Variety's premier honour. They were the first *couple* to share the Award. The President of Variety International said, 'They are a constant reminder to us of what can be achieved for the suffering and helpless through selfless dedication and compassionate devotion,' Sue Ryder received a further honour in 1976 when, in the Queen's Birthday Honours, she was named Knight Commander of the Most Honourable Order of St Michael and St George.

As Sue Ryder's work has developed, so also the work of the Cheshire Foundation is constantly expanding. It does not develop according to any pre-conceived plan, but as and when the need and opportunity arise. From the beginning of his personal mission of compassion, Cheshire has been guided by two simple principles: 'No genuine call for help will be ignored. No genuine offer of help will be refused.'

A man does not change his nature with his religion. In Cheshire's case, the brilliant and versatile attributes he formerly devoted to fighting for his own country, he has since dedicated to serving people of all nations. He sees a close connection between Christian mission and the care of the sick and disabled. He says, 'They are both concerned with suffering —the one to relieve it, the other to make its significance understood. In order to understand suffering, we have to understand Christ, for it is Christ alone who explains it. Without Christ, suffering remains a horrible and meaningless misfortune.' [5]

There are those who will remember Leonard Cheshire as a daring RAF pilot who acted as the *pathfinder* for so many successful bombing raids and who won the highest awards possible for gallantry in time of war. There will be many more who will remember him as a *pathfinder* of a very different kind—the man who has searched out areas of human need and then sought to bring help and healing. One of those who will never forget him is an old woman who, desperately ill, was taken to one of his centres in India. There she was nursed back to health by Cheshire himself. When the time came for her to return home, she asked one of the nursing staff what she might send to express her gratitude to 'the wonderful Captain'. The nurse replied, 'Mr Cheshire, you mean? Nothing, nothing at all.' 'Oh, but I must send him something', said the old Indian woman. 'Something to show that I remember what he has done for me.' The nurse shook her head and said, 'You must not think of it like that. It is all a service for Jesus. We all do it in service for Jesus.' [6]

Definition of a Cheshire Home approved at the 21st Anniversary International Conference of Cheshire Foundations, July 1969:

'A Cheshire Home should be a place of shelter physically, and of encouragement spiritually; a place in which the residents can acquire a sense of belonging and of ownership to contributing in any way within their capabilities to its functioning and development; a place to share with others, and from which to help others less fortunate; a place in which to gain confidence and develop independence and interests; a place of hopeful endeavour and not of passive disinterest.'

*   *   *

References

Grateful acknowledgement is made to the Author and Publisher of 'No Passing Glory' by Andrew Boyle: Wm Collins Sons & Co. Ltd, 1955.

1. p. 77.   2. p. 85.   3. p. 96.   4. p. 213.   5. p. 337.
6. p. 369.

For Further Reading

Biographies

'Cheshire, V.C.': Russell Braddon: Evans Bros. Ltd, 1954; Arrow Books Ltd., 1966

'No Passing Glory': Andrew Boyle: Wm Collins Sons & Co. Ltd, 1955

'Leonard Cheshire, V.C.'—Living Biographies for Young People: Cledwyn Hughes: Phoenix House, 1961

'The Pilot Who Changed Course'—Biography for To-day Series: Carolyn Scott: Lutterworth Press, 1972

See also:

'The Dam Busters'—the story of 617 Squadron, the RAF: Paul Brickhill: Evans Bros Ltd, 1951; Pan Books Ltd, 1954

The Cheshire Homes

'New Lives For Old': Wilfred Russell: Victor Gollancz Ltd, 1963
'The Cheshire Homes—A Pictorial Record': Cheshire Foundation Homes, 1963
'Cheshire Smile'—the quarterly magazine of the Cheshire Homes

Books by Group Captain Leonard Cheshire

'Bomber Pilot': Hutchinson, 1943
'The Holy Face': Johns Press, 1954
'Pilgrimage to the Shroud': Hutchinson, 1956
'Face of Victory': Hutchinson, 1961

Miss Sue Ryder, C.M.G., O.B.E.—Biography

'But Some There Be': A.J. Forrest: Robert Hale Ltd

Films

Bookings should be made only to the Secretary, Cheshire Foundation Homes. Hire charges payable to Religious Films Ltd, Foundation House, Walton Road, Bushey, Watford, WD2 2JF

'Pathfinder': the growth of the Cheshire Homes in the U.K. and the start of the work overseas: BBC TV 1959. B/w. 50 mins.

'Living Waters': the founding of Homes for the Sick in India: 1968. Col. 24 mins.

'Share Thy Bread': the first joint venture of Leonard Cheshire and Sue Ryder in India for the homeless and disabled: Col. 18 mins.

'Dar El Hanna': first Cheshire Home in Morocco for crippled children: Col. 25 mins.

'A Small Child Singing': Cheshire's first visit to the six West African Homes, all for crippled children: 1965. Col. 21 mins.

'First Cheshire Home in New Guinea': the first steps in building a home for mentally and physically handicapped children in Papua New Guinea: Col. 25 mins.

'The Weakest Link': the growth of the Homes in Ireland: B/w. 16 mins.

'Let Me Live': the starting of St Teresa's the second Cheshire Home, and the formation of the Trust: Col. 35 mins.

'On a Cold and Frosty Morning': the International Ryder-Cheshire Centre at Dehra Dun in N. India. Col. 16 mins.

'The Fifth Gospel': the story of the Holy Shroud of Turin: B/w. 20 mins.

'To Be A Pilgrim': a day in the life of a pilgrim at Lourdes: Col. 25 mins.

'A Man and a House': a filmed sequence of 'stills' showing the development of Le Court. Col. 15 mins.

'Dilip': the authentic story of a boy who discovered at the age of twelve that he had leprosy: Col. 27 mins.

'Yvonne—A Room of Her Own': a severely disabled person thinks back when at last she gets her wish—a room of her own: Col. 20 mins.

'A Place Called Home': two residents in a Cheshire Home discuss their life and the Homes in general: Col. 20 mins.

'A House by a Church': the Cheshire Home at Staunton Harold: Col. 30 mins.

Additional Films which can be hired from Concord Films Ltd, Nacton, Ipswich, Suffolk, IP10 OJZ (who can supply some of the films mentioned above):

'Living Proof': Le Court and its disabled residents: 1966. Col. 25 mins.

'Challenge': Le Court and Mary Marlborough Lodge, Oxford, shows how the severely disabled tackle their handicaps: 1967. Col. 27 mins.

'No Limit': about Le Court and its people: Col. 20 mins.

'Away from Dependence': the work in Manila in the Philippines: 1974. Col. 30 mins.

'Where Courage Lives': the Homes in the Far East: 1974. Col. 30 mins.

'Maybe Today—Le Court': produced by the Le Court Film Unit: 1974. Col. 12 mins.

For Further Information

Full details of these films and of Video Tape Programmes featuring the Leonard Cheshire Foundation, for use in schools, youth clubs, churches, etc., may be obtained from the Secretary, The Leonard Cheshire Foundation, 7 Market Mews, London W1Y 8HP.

CHAPTER SIX

Don Vesuvio of Naples

Mario Borrelli

Born 1922

'Out in the streets there were kids of seven or eight years old with nowhere to sleep, hundreds of them in the rain and wind, fighting for the privilege of lying by the grating of a baker's shop that would give them a little warmth, kids for whom one sheet of newspaper was as good as a blanket, and their only pillow another lad's ribs.'[1]   These are the words of Mario Borrelli, written when he was an Italian Roman Catholic priest. He refers to the *scugnizzi*, the boy street urchins of Naples. Father Borrelli was himself born in the Neapolitan slums, the youngest of a poor family of ten children, five of whom died in infancy. He went to work in a barber's shop when he was only eight years old. At thirteen he knew he wanted to become a priest. Don Nobilione, one of the barber's customers, himself a priest, offered to pay for Mario to go to school. After the first year, Don Nobilione could no longer afford to pay the school fees and so Mario's mother went out to work to pay for a further four years' schooling. When he was eighteen, Mario entered a theological seminary and in 1946 he was ordained a priest. The conditions he found in post-war Naples angered him, particularly the plight of the homeless children. 'I knew that I could not remain a priest', he said, 'unless I did something worthy of a priest. I could not stand at the altar and hold the body of God in my hands while the bodies of his children slept in the alleys and under the barrows in the Mercato.'[2]

Mario Borrelli decided that before he could help the *scugnizzi* he would have to win their confidence and to do this he must become one of them. With some difficulty he obtained permission for his unusual mission, and one evening in 1950, he exchanged his priest's cassock for the tattered clothes of a *scugnizzo*. He made his way to the Vasto district which had become the gathering place for the *scugnizzi* of Naples. The group of boys he approached looked warily at this new arrival. He wore a filthy patched shirt, ragged trousers, odd shoes, a faded scarf and a greasy peaked cap. He sat down to smoke the cigarette-end he had just picked from the gutter. The ringleader of the onlookers, O Chiattone (Fatty), went over to the disguised priest and tapped him on the head. 'Come on, now,' he said, 'who are you?' Mario Borrelli rose slowly and spat in his face. 'That's who I am', he snarled. The gang went silent. Borrelli's left hand went swiftly to his pocket as if for a knife, and with his right hand he caught O Chiattone by the arm. O Chiattone grinned sourly and from his pocket pulled a razor blade which he handed to Borrelli. 'I'd have carved you', he said, 'but you got your hand in your pocket before I did. So here you are.' The gift of the razor blade was the mark of acceptance. Father Borrelli had overcome his first hurdle, he was now one of the *scugnizzi*.

So began the young priest's bizarre double-life. His nights were spent on the street and during the day, often nodding with fatigue, he fulfilled his duties as a teacher and priest. When he disappeared in the early hours of the morning, the *scugnizzi* assumed that he was going into the city centre to 'work' the trams as a pickpocket. To gain the confidence of the gang he had to share their activities. He kept watch while his companions burgled. He peddled cigarettes, he acted with the others as a pimp, he ate bread bought with money stolen from Church poor boxes, he became a beggar. He carried bags for the tourists, whined for cigarettes and collected trodden butts— removing the tobacco to sell to the back-alley cigarette manufacturers.

This was the most difficult part of Don Borrelli's new life. The man of God had to act as a petty criminal. For the sake of conscience he tried to confine himself to the fringe of law-breaking, giving as convincing a performance as he could when he was with the *scugnizzi*. Then, about midnight he would sit with them around a fire and share the scraps of food they had managed to acquire. Sometimes he joined the queue for food and a drink from the Salvation Army van. He slept under a stairway, in a porch or on the pavement.

During the time Father Borrelli lived with the *scugnizzi*, he was planning how best he could help them. Watching them at night, hungry and shivering with cold, he knew that their most urgent need was food and shelter. He knew he must find a way to give them security with freedom, building on the bond that their shared suffering gave them. He must obtain vitamins and drugs to treat those who were undernourished and ill. Later he must try to educate them and find them work.

One night, as the gang huddled together for warmth, Nino, one of the youngest members, began to tremble violently. 'What's the matter?' asked Borrelli, 'I'm cold, Mario. I'm cold', said the little boy. Borrelli took him in his arms. Nino's thin body was racked with a spasm of coughing. His vomit was stained with blood. Mario Borrelli knew he was holding a child in an advanced stage of tuberculosis. The others watched him. Somehow they felt that this Mario was different, he seemed to care about them.

Realising that he had now won their confidence, Father Borrelli decided that the time had come to start implementing his plans. The next day he disappeared, saying that he was going to beg medicine for Nino. A friend from his seminary days, Ciccio—now Don Spada—had been searching for a building where the street urchins could be sheltered. He told Mario the good news that he had discovered an abandoned church which they could get permission to use. Although bomb damaged, the little church of Saint Gennaro a Materdei had a roof and sound walls. With the help of Ciccio and two other friends, Vittoria—a young school teacher and Pasquale— another priest, the walls were whitewashed and all rubbish removed. Then they begged for blankets, straw to make mattresses, cooking utensils, food and clothes.

Father Borrelli, wished to get the 'home' established before revealing his true identity to the *scugnizzi*, so he sent Vittorio to invite two or three of them to the shelter of the renovated Church. One little boy came and after a couple of nights, vanished. Pasquale then went out and had more success. At last the empty building began to resound with the shouts and laughter of children. Mario Borrelli decided that they should now attempt to draw in his own gang. However, he still did not wish to disclose himself for fear they should feel tricked. So, for several nights, another friend, Salvatore—a photographer— visited the haunts of the *scugnizzi* and talked to them about the disused church of Saint Gennaro a Materdei where they might be given shelter. He told them it was run by a priest known as 'Don Vesuvio' (the volcano). Little did they know that the *scugnizzo* who urged them to follow Salvatore's advice was 'Don Vesuvio' himself. Some time after midnight, Don Pasquale answered a knock on the door of the Materdei and admitted Mario (whom he pretended not to recognize) and nine of his boys.

As the number of those seeking shelter grew, it became necessary to earn money to buy food. Vittorio, the school-teacher, managed to acquire a hand-cart. With this the boys were sent out to collect scrap-iron, discarded clothes and anything that could be sold at a profit. Soon the hand-cart was replaced by a donkey-cart, and later by a lorry. Within a little while the Casa dello Scugnizzo, as it became known, was providing shelter and employment for a large number of young boys. Father Borrelli now felt the time was ripe to attempt to bring in the older and tougher *scugnizzi*. There were fewer boys in the Vasta district now; those remaining had begun to join an older gang who haunted the San Carlo Theatre and the Galleria Umberto opposite. When Father Borrelli found their hide-out, he was greeted with suspicion and hostility. After a brief conversation, their leader, Cicillo, set about Borrelli, driving him off with kicks and blows. Salvatore then volunteered to go to the gang to act as a 'go between'. He found them and began to talk about 'Don Vesuvio's place'. When Father Borrelli, still dressed as a *scugnizzo* drifted up, Salvatore explained that the new arrival knew this 'Don Vesuvio' and could bring him along to meet them. As they talked, Salvatore took photogaphs of the group, making sure Father Borrelli was included. A few days later, on Easter Saturday, the *Il Granellino*, a parish church paper, was published. On the front cover was one of Salvatore's photographs of the disguised Borrelli with the gang. That evening, dressed as a priest, Father Borrelli went with Salvatore to find the same gang. He was introduced as 'Don Vesuvio'. No-one recognised him. The *scugnizzi* eagerly examined the picture, identifying each other. Cicillo, their leader, looked closely at one unidentified figure on the photograph. 'That's the one I kicked out', he said. Then he looked at Mario Borrelli in astonishment and said, 'Is that *you*—Father?' 'Yes, I'm "Don Vesuvio" ', the priest replied. There was a long pause while the information sank in and they grasped the significance of what Borrelli had done. Suddenly the *scugnizzi* were all over him, trying to kiss him, shake his hand. Later, Father Borrelli wrote, 'They were young toughs—but then they were also Neapolitans. They knew that what I had done I had done with love, and they knew instinctively, though they could never have said it, that that was what they most needed.' [3]

For seven months Mario Borrelli had played a double role, that of schoolmaster-priest by day and street urchin by night. Now he could return openly to the Materdei church and reveal his true identity to the younger boys already in residence. At the Casa dello Scugnizzo—The House of the Urchins, the boys found food, a mattress to lie on and a roof over their heads; but, above all, they found kindness and a sense of being wanted and cared for. This first 'Casa', which came into being in 1951, had room for only forty boys, a small fraction of the total number of *scugnizzi*.

For the next ten years Father Borrelli had to devise a variety of fund-raising projects to ensure the survival of the Casa. He organised organ concerts, cinema shows, theatre plays, funfairs, raffles, sporting events and carnivals. He also became a concessionary for the sale of national lottery tickets in Naples and Caserta. His association with the Society for the Concessionaries of National Lotteries proved most advantageous, for in 1951 the winning ticket for the First Prize in the National Lottery of Agnano was not sold and the Society decided to donate most of the 40.000.000 lira to the Casa. With this money Father Borrelli was able to purchase the site of the old church of S. Gennaro, and it was on this land that the new premises were eventually built.

Gradually the work of the Casa became more widely known, helped particularly by the publication in 1957 of an account of Father Borrelli's work by Morris West entitled, *Children of the Sun*. Support from overseas came first from Australia, then Britain, and, during the next few years, from many other nations. Father Borrelli's own book, *A Street Lamp and the Stars*, was published in Britain in 1963, and a film was made about his work, called, *'Naples the Anonymous'*. He himself travelled abroad giving lectures, talks and interviews as well as broadcasting on radio and television.

In Naples, church and civil authorities were by now awakened to the needs of the *scugnizzi*. Social and medical workers, the police and lay volunteers began to co-operate in the work of the Casa. The boys were encouraged to live as normal a life as possible—attending school, being taught a trade, being helped to find employment. Some of them were assisted to emigrate to Britain, the United States of America, Switzerland and elsewhere, making a new start in very different surroundings to those of their childhood. The rehabilitation of the *scugnizzi* was not always successful, however, and Father Borrelli writes of the failures, 'These can hurt, but they can never dismay or discourage me. Even if they were numerous, what could it matter in comparison with one ragged little unloved thief taken out of the gutter and turned into a well-integrated and decent member of society?' [4]

To achieve a greater measure of financial security, Father Borrelli joined a religious community, the Congregation of the Oratory, which became the custodian of the Casa, with himself as the Director. Each morning he worked as Librarian of the Oratory Library, a State appointment which provided a personal salary on which he was able to support himself and his mother, without having to draw on Casa income.

Although a second Casa was acquired which accommodated another forty boys, Father Borrelli realised that the problem of the *scugnizzi* had its roots in the poverty-stricken homes and broken families from which they originated. Many of these families lived in the barrache, the shanty towns which had grown up on bomb sites and on waste land along the waterfront of Naples. Approximately twenty-five thousand people existed in huts made from scrap materials, without either a proper water supply or adequate sanitation. Father Borrelli handed over the day-to-day running of the Casas to two qualified social workers and, in 1960, he went to live in a shack in one of the shanty towns. This time he made no attempt to conceal his true identity. By moving there he gained first-hand knowledge of living conditions in a shanty town. He also hoped that his action would draw national attention to the squalor in which so many families were forced to live.

Inspired by Father Borrelli's example, a number of Groups of volunteers went to different areas of the shanty towns to befriend, advise, and encourage the barrache dwellers to overcome their own problems. The majority of the volunteers were young people aged between sixteen and twenty, who came from all walks of life. Educational, recreational and religious activities were organised for children and adults. A Group comprising lecturers and students from the University of Naples assisted Father Borrelli by making a statistical survey of the living conditions of every family in one shanty town. A Committee was formed, of which Father Borrelli was a member, to pressurise the city authorities to act in such urgent matters as clearing the main drains, exterminating rats, providing a mains water supply and building proper houses. Father Borrelli also took part in a Group Hunger-fast and in several Protest Marches organised by the Committee.

The publicity achieved by these means, plus the facts disclosed in the survey, influenced the local authorities to embark on a building programme which enabled five hundred families to be re-housed in two years. Father Borrelli then moved on to another shanty area and used the same tactics to bring about another re-housing programme. Within six years the barrache was demolished and the former population moved to new apartment blocks. Unfortunately, as in so many schemes of mass re-housing in many other countries, the apartment blocks were situated outside the city boundary, at a distance from sources of employment and without shopping, medical or recreational facilities. Worst of all, there were so few schools that the children could only attend in three shifts of two hours each day. Consequently, although families were better housed, the children still spent much of their time on the streets.

Meanwhile, the work of the Casa had been growing. By 1967, the overseas supporting Committees for the House of Urchins Fund had raised £120,000 to build a new Casa. The new Casa, built on the site of the old Materdei Church, is an imposing four-storeyed building, standing in the midst of dilapidated slum property. The opening ceremony took place on 22 December 1969. The new Casa dello Scugnizzo was planned as a Community Centre which would be able to serve the needs of whole families. The broad aim would be 'to help in every way young people who were socially, physically or psychologically maladjusted. Whilst a number of boys would live in the new Casa, as they had lived in the old one, every effort would now be made to restore children to their families whenever possible; the emphasis being on the family as a unit, rather than on only one member of it.' [5] With the help of a team of experts in various fields of social welfare a wide range of community services was planned. At first, however, the Casa was inclined to be a small and rather specialised community with a tendency to emphasise the difference between its members and the rest of society, and unable to provide accommodation or opportunities for the many girls who were no less in need than the boys.

At this point in his career, Father Borrelli felt the need for some further academic training and, from 1968 to 1970, studied in England at the London School of Economics for a degree in Social Administration. This course was the foundation of his work when he returned to Italy. In October 1970 he resigned from the priesthood and since then has been known simply as Signor Mario Borrelli. It was a hard decision to take, but Borrelli felt that so long as he was regarded as part of the hierarchical structure of the Church, he would be handicapped in his work with the underprivileged, most of whom were suspicious and resentful of anyone who represented 'authority'. Furthermore, he believed that by becoming a layman he would have more freedom of speech and action, and would be less likely to cause embarrassment to the Church if he was involved in any militant action against the civic authorities. He had become convinced that it was the community as a whole—not merely the Church— which ought to accept its social responsibilities, 'and it is natural', he wrote, 'that I should take part in this community on the same conditions as the others'. [6] He emphasised that he was not renouncing the Church and that leaving the priesthood was not 'an act of despair against the social incapacity of the Church, but is really an act of faith in the social conscience of the Christian community'. [7] On 19 September 1971 he married Miss Jilyan West, who worked as a secretary at the Southern European Command of the NATO Forces in Naples.

Although the needs of boys in the one to fourteen years age group was still his main interest, Signor Borrelli gradually widened the scope of the work done at the new Casa. In 1974, the 'Casa dello Scugnizzo' became the 'Centro Communitario Materdei' (the 'Materdei Community Centre'), a name which reflects the changed emphasis of the work. There is no longer a group of boys resident at the Casa; most of its rooms are now used by the Local Authority to operate welfare services which are essential to the neighbourhood but beyond the funds available to Borrelli. Thus, the Centre now houses a nursery school for 120 infants, an elementary school for 250 children, and an evening school for adults, all provided at the expense of the Commune of Naples. In addition, Signor Borrelli organises other equally necessary services. There are classes at the Centre for 150 children who are educationally retarded or do not attend school; they come with their mothers and younger brothers and sisters and they are all given free meals. The Centre also provides a medical clinic, a legal aid scheme, a service of advice on social and family problems, recreational activities such as a music school and the Excelsior sports club, and the provision of money, food and clothing in cases of special need. Signor Borrelli and his team of full-time and voluntary workers seek to involve the whole community of the Materdei district in working for its own improvement. It is hoped that, as time passes,

> 'responsible people will emerge from the community to express their own needs and to organise their own services in conjunction with the Centre, leading to a community development programme that can be politically effective in demanding from the City Authorities the standards of housing and quality of life that are at present enjoyed only in the more favoured parts of Naples'. [8]

A tremendous amount of good has been achieved by Mario Borrelli since he became one of the *scugnizzi* in 1950. However, he is painfully aware of the poverty, bad housing and juvenile delinquency which remains unconquered in Naples. But, as he says, 'It is better to light a match than to swear against the darkness.' He has many ideas for the future: one of them is a plan to concentrate on the needs of very young children in an effort to prevent them becoming the *scugnizzi* of tomorrow.

Although no longer an ordained and separated priest, Mario Borrelli knows himself to be one of the 'priesthood of *all* believers'. His motivation remains the same as it was when, newly ordained, he stood before Cardinal Ascalesi, Archbishop of Naples, and sought to justify his extraordinary request to become one of the street urchins.

'Ever since I entered the seminary,' he wrote, 'I have been

taught that a priest must make himself "alter Christus"—
another Christ. It is written in the gospels that Christ ate
and drank with thieves and street women. How can a priest
be wrong if he does the same? How can he be another
Christ if he refuses to go down to those who have no
shepherd?' [9]

References

Grateful acknowledgement is made to the Authors and Publishers of the
literature cited below:

1. SLAS, p. 71.   2. COS, p. 83.   3. SLAS, p. 185.   4. SLAS, p. 206.
5. MB, p. 31.   6. CDSN, No. 32, April 1971, p.1
7. CDSN, No. 32, April 1971, p. 2.   8. MB, p. 33.   9. COS, p. 85.

For Further Reading

Children of the Sun': Morris West: Heinemann, 1957 (COS)

A Street Lamp and the Stars': Mario Borrelli and Anthony Thorne: Peter
Davies, London, 1963 (SLAS)

Mario Borrelli': Peter Hargreaves: West Yorkshire and Lindsey Examining
Board, 1973 (MB)

The Defiant Ones—Dramatic Studies—Borrelli, Dolci': Brian Peachment:
R.E.P., 1974

Children of Naples'—Faith in Action Series: Geoffrey Hanks: R.E.P., 1974

Casa Dello Scugnizzo News': Editor: Largo S. Gennaro (CDSN)

Films

Naples the Anonymous': B/w. Obtainable from the British House of Urchins
Fund (address below)

The Sun Casts A Shadow'—International Help for Children organises holidays
in Britain for under-privileged children, including some from the Casa
Dello Scugnizzo: B/w. 20 mins. Obtainable from Concord Films Council,
Nacton, Ipswich, Suffolk IP10 OJZ

For Further Information

The Secretary, British House of Urchins Fund, Miss M.S.L. Clark, 26 Hanover
House, High Street, St John's Wood, London NW8.

The Secretary, Centro Communitaris Materdei, Casella Postale N. 378, Napoli,
Italy.

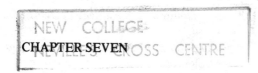

CHAPTER SEVEN

Prisoner on the Railway of Death

Ernest Gordon

Born 1922

As the sun dipped below the horizon, the *Setia Berganti*, a small Malayan fishing boat, headed out to sea. It was April 1942, Singapore had fallen to the Japanese Army, Sumatra was about to fall. Ten British Commonwealth Servicemen were making a desperate bid to escape by sea to Ceylon. Among them was Ernest Gordon, a twenty-four-year-old Captain in the Argyll and Sutherland Highlanders. He was a Scotsman who had been brought up at Dunoon on the Firth of Clyde. At the outbreak of war in 1939, he was on vacation from the University of Saint Andrews. He was commissioned in the Army, and in the late autumn embarked with first-line reinforcements for service overseas.

After being in action in France, he was posted to Malaya where he joined the Second Battalion of the Argyll and Sutherland Highlanders. When the Japanese attacked, the Argylls went into battle and fought a courageous rear-guard action through the dense jungle. On 30 December 1942 they retreated to Singapore Island to make a last stand. There they fought until the Garrison had completely run out of drinking water and ammunition.

Of the thousand-strong battalion that had set out from Britain, only thirty or so were left. Ernest and a few others commandeered a ferry and crossed the Straits to Sumatra. There the senior officer was organising an official escape party; Ernest was invited to join it. With money given by the Dutch, the prahu *Setia Berganti* was purchased and the ten officers set sail for Colombo.

Their bid for freedom was shortlived. Within five hundred miles of their goal the *Setia Berganti* was sighted by three Japanese ships. One of them fired a shot across the prahu's bows, and the escapees had no choice but to surrender. Four days later Ernest was back in Singapore and on his way to Changi, a prison camp on the east side of the Island. To his great joy, he found the survivors of his battalion established in a corner of the prison area. But his personal troubles were not over. After a violent attack of malaria he became ill with appendicitis. An operation was urgently necessary and was performed by the light of a kerosene lamp, with Ernest lying on a rough kitchen table. Within three days he rejoined his comrades. He found that morale was very low. The humiliation of their defeat and surrender, the brutal treatment by their captors, and the wretched inadequacy of their food all contributed to the general feeling of deep depression. Some of the prisoners had turned to religion, but it appeared to Ernest that many of them were motivated from fear rather than from genuine faith.

After a few weeks, the Argylls were moved to a smaller camp at Banpong in Thailand. There the officers tried to combat apathy and listlessness by holding Saturday-night vaudevilles, but the attempt met with little success. In September, the prisoners were marched to a new camp, Chungkai, on the banks of the River Kwai. Here they were given what seemed an impossible task—to build, in less than twelve months, a railway several hundred miles in length to be used for transporting Japanese troops to the Burmese front. In addition, a bridge had to be constructed to carry a railroad over the river. Seven days a week the prisoners were marched out of Chungkai to hack out a permanent way for the railway. They usually worked from early morning until late at night, either in heat that often reached 120°F, or in the torrential rain of the monsoons. Human life was cheap. Men collapsed from exhaustion, starvation and disease, or from the merciless beatings of their overseers. The project became known as the Railway of Death. As conditions worsened, the atmosphere of the camp was slowly poisoned by selfishness, hate and fear. Men, normally decent and generous, lived by the law of the jungle. The weak were brushed aside, the sick ignored, the dead forgotten. With a few exceptions, it was a case of every man for himself. Those who at Changi had turned to religion as a crutch, now became disillusioned. They had no chaplain, no church, no services of worship—and seemingly, no God.

Ernest Gordon was not only afflicted by this malaise of spirit but also became desperately ill physically. He was already suffering from the effects of malaria, dysentery, beri-beri and the appendicectomy, when he contracted diphtheria. The Medical Officer diagnosed polyneuritis, a consequence of diphtheria, and he was sent to the camp 'hospital', known to the prisoners as the Death House. It was the monsoon season, and the floor of the hut was a sea of mud. The sick lay on filthy wooden platforms; they were already too ill to be helped by the limited medical treatment that was available, and they were taken there simply to die. Like Ernest, most of them were too weak to care; death was seen as an escape to be welcomed. Few of the other prisoners came to visit them, consequently Ernest was surprised one day to see two prisoners approaching whom he recognised. They were two Argylls who had only recently arrived at the Camp, and had come to the Death House looking for him. They failed to recognise his emaciated figure and would have gone away had he not managed to attract the attention of an orderly who called them back. Shortly after their visit, Ernest asked to be moved to that part of the hut used as a morgue—there, at least, it was cleaner, the air was fresher and the ground dry to lie on.

A few days later, however, one of his friends received permission to move Ernest to a little hut which some of his fellow officers had built. The Medical Officer told them that there was no hope of Ernest recovering, but it was their wish that he should spend his last days in more pleasant surroundings than the morgue. They carried him carefully to the hut and left him half-dozing on a bed they had made from split bamboo.

During the evening Ernest awoke to see a prisoner he did not recognise standing in the doorway. The man spoke in a soft north-country voice, 'Good evening, sir. I heard that you needed a hand and I wondered if you'd care to let me help you?' Ernest was impresed by his easy, friendly manner and invited him in. 'Dusty' Miller, as he was known, then fetched warm water and gave his new patient a thorough wash; afterwards he cleaned the ulcerated sores on Ernest's legs. The next day, Dennis Moore, known as 'Dinty', a former school friend, came to offer his help too. Together, Dusty and Dinty achieved what seemed impossible—they gave their patient a will to live. With infinite care and patience they nursed him back to health and then taught him to walk again. Although they were men of very different temperament, Ernest was interested to discover that they had one thing in common—each possessed a deep Christian faith.

When, at last, he was able to get about the camp on his own, Ernest found that, in some inexplicable way, the atmosphere had begun to change. Stores were circulating of acts of self-sacrifice, heroism and kindness. Generosity was evidently contagious for men were beginning to think less of themselves and more of their fellows.

One day, as Dusty Miller bathed Ernest's ulcerated legs, their talk turned to the meaning of life and death. Dusty expressed his conviction that God had a purpose for every individual. 'Then why', asked Ernest, 'doesn't he do something, instead of sitting quiescently on a great big white throne in the no-place called heaven?' 'Maybe he does', Dusty replied, and went on to quote a verse of poetry:

> ' "No one could tell me where my soul might be;
> I sought for God, but God eluded me;
> I sought my *brother* out and found all three—
> My soul, my God, and all humanity." '

The next day, Dusty returned with a Bible and read from the New Testament the passage which begins: 'There is no fear in love . . .' and concludes '. . . This commandment have we from

him, that he who loveth God, loves his brother also' (1 John 4
18-21). Ernest lay back and considered what he had heard. He
knew these verses contained truth because both Dusty and
Dinty lived by them. In his book, *Miracle on the River Kwai*,
Ernest Gordon recalls the significance of that realisation; he
writes:

> 'For the first time I understood. Dusty was a Methodist
> —Dinty a Roman Catholic. Yet in each it was his faith that
> lent a special grace to his personality; through them both
> faith expressed a power, a presence, greater than them-
> selves. I was beginning to see that life was infinitely more
> complex, and at the same time more wonderful, than I had
> ever imagined. True, there was hatred. But there was also
> love. There was death. But there was also life. God had not
> left us. He was with us, calling us to live the divine life in
> fellowship. I was beginning to be aware of the miracle that
> God was working in the Death Camp by the River Kwai.'[1]

Ernest began to ask himself why *he* was so uncommitted.
While he wrestled with his conflicting thoughts, an Australian
sergeant approached him with a request from a group of
Australian soldiers who were keen to discuss the claims of
Christianity. Ernest protested that he was hardly suitable to
lead a *religious* discussion; however, the sergeant insisted
saying, 'My cobbers think you're right for the job. They know
you're a fighting soldier. Also, you've been to University.' With
such limited qualifications, Ernest found himself the next
evening facing a group of several dozen men. All he had to draw
on was a battered, and hitherto unused, Bible. He began by
describing frankly his own doubts and conflicts and then
invited questions. One by one, this group of hardened soldiers
confessed their own problems of belief. Before they parted it
was agreed to carry on meeting while they searched for a
religious faith that was relevant to their situation.

At each successive meeting the numbers attending grew.
Ernest did his best to expound the New Testament in language
that the ordinary soldier would understand. Gradually he

became conscious of a change taking place within *himself* as well as in those who came to debate together. He recalls that:

> 'Through our reading and discussions we gradually came to know Jesus. He was one of us. He would understand our problems, because they were the kind of problems he faced himself. . . . As we read and talked, he became flesh and blood. . . . We arrived at our understanding of God's ways not one by one, but together. In the fellowship of freedom and love we found truth; and with truth a wonderful sense of unity, of harmony, of peace.' [2]

The Australian sergeant had already formed a team of volunteers who gave massage treatment to those prisoners whose legs were paralysed. Ernest joined this team and found that, apart from the benefits of massage, his 'patients' appreciated having someone to confide in. Most of them were young, many of them were seriously ill with little hope of recovery; they all had one over-riding question: 'How do I face death?' Ernest found that the message he tried to impart concerning a God who had experienced suffering through the crucifixion of his son, Jesus Christ, and who, in Christ, had overcome death, was deeply meaningful.

A new spirit of faith and hope began to spread through the camp, a feeling expressed in the increased concern that the prisoners had for one another. Many prisoners had lost legs as a result of tropical ulcers and other diseases caused by malnutrition. These men were among the most dispirited until a cobbler and an engineer got together and improvised an artificial leg from odds and ends of scrap material. Under their direction a new 'industry' developed. The legless themselves were taught to make artificial limbs, and later, to make sandals for those who had legs.

To meet a growing hunger for education, a 'jungle-university' came into being. Those with a specialised knowledge were enlisted to lead seminars in a variety of subjects. Men pooled what books they had in order to create a lending library. There was a spontaneous outburst of artistic activity culminating in an exhibition of cartoons, painting and sculpture. An orchestra was formed and, although many of the instruments were home-made, regular concerts became one of the most valued features of camp life. Drama, dance and community-singing also helped to refresh the spirits of men whose bodies were impoverished through hard labour, disease and malnutrition.

The new-found faith in God which an increasing number of prisoners shared resulted in a strengthening of the resolve to survive. Self-respect increased because human life was seen to have value once more. Stealing ceased, mutual trust grew, and there was an end to the suspicion and selfishness which previously had poisoned the common life of the camp. A clearing in the jungle became recognised as the prisoners' 'Church'; its roof was the sky, its walls the forest of bamboo; the only requirement for membership was the confession of Jesus Christ as Lord. Apart from Sunday worship, every evening a service was held at which prayers were said for the sick, for those at home, and for their own daily needs. On Christmas Day 1943 over two thousand POW's filled the church to sing the familiar carols and to hear a brief sermon on 'the *hope* of Christmas'. The atmosphere among the men was strikingly different from that of the previous Christmas. One of the prisoners remarked how everyone seemed much more hopeful, even though the prospect of release was no nearer. Ernest commented that besides hope there was an altogether *new* spirit in the camp. 'Have you noticed,' he said, 'how with many of the men, it's "*you* first" now instead of "*me* first "?' 3

The infamous bridge over the River Kwai and the railway that had claimed so many lives was completed. The other camps, higher up the rail-route, were emptied and Chungkai became a transit camp for those prisoners who had managed to survive. The following Autumn, Ernest Gordon was moved to the Nakawm Paton camp in Burma, a camp mainly for the sick. This camp was a depressing contrast to Chungkai, but Ernest and some of his fellow-prisoners from Chungkai decided to do what they could to overcome the general air of listlessness and defeat. They organised a blood transfusion service and formed a team of masseurs. Once again they set about the task of helping those who had given up hope to discover a reason for living. They held meetings for fellowship and worship and gradually a few others began to meet with them. The appearance of the camp began to improve. The living quarters were cleaned, men began to help one another; the less sick cared for the more sick, those able to walk fetched water and washed those unable to wash themselves. Looking back on these events, Ernest Gordon writes:

> 'I realised that I was witnessing the same saving grace at work here that had redeemed many of us at Changkai. In some way the change taking place at Nakawm Paton was even more wonderful. Since this was a hospital camp, the hopelessness had been acute. Indeed, it had been so complete that men did not trouble to steal from each other. So many wanted to do nothing but die. Now there was a stirring of hope, and, with hope, a feeling among many that life was worth living.' [4]

Ernest continued to be regarded as a Christian leader among the prisoners. On Christmas Day 1944, in his third year of captivity, he was asked to preach to a congregation of many nationalities which overflowed the hut used as a church. A more difficult service for them all was that on Good Friday, when they attended a Roman Catholic service which followed the 'Stations of the Cross'. They were reminded of Christ's words, 'Father, forgive them, for they know not what they do.' This was no easy prayer for a prisoner to make for they were often treated with excessive brutality. For instance, on one occasion, a British prisoner, who acted as an interpreter, tried to protect an officer who was being tortured. The Japanese Camp Commandant, noted for his vicious cruelty, had the interpreter seized, and himself beat him senseless before having him thrown into a trench with orders that he be left there. It was indeed hard for them to love their enemies and to pray for them.

After some weeks, orders were given to move the whole camp

to an area north-east of Bangkok. At one stage of the journey by train, Ernest Gordon and his contingent of prisoners were shunted into a siding along with several trucks of wounded Japanese soldiers. The Japanese were in a shocking state. Their uniforms were encrusted with mud, blood and excrement, their undressed wounds crawled with maggots. They had been left alone with no medical care. Without any prompting, most of the officers in Ernest's section went over to the Japanese train and, using their own limited rations, they gave them food and water and dressed their wounds. The prisoners' own guards tried to stop this spontaneous demonstration of compassion, shouting 'No Goodka! No goodka!' But Ernest and his men continued to do what they could to bring comfort and relief. Then an Allied Officer from another section of the train came and protested, 'What bloody fools you all are. Don't you realise that those are the enemy?' Ernest replied by reminding him of the story of the Good Samaritan. 'But that's different,' the officer retorted angrily. 'That's in the Bible. They are the swine who've starved us and beaten us. They've murdered our comrades. These are our enemies.' Ernest replied, 'God makes neighbours; *we* make enemies. . . . My enemy *is* my neighbour' [5] The officer turned away in disgust and left Ernest to marvel at the fact that eighteen months previously, the same men who had just dressed the wounds of their enemies, if given the chance, would have killed them outright. God had indeed worked a miracle.

Eventually, after marching forty miles in tropical rain, the prisoners reached Camp Nakon Nyok. This was not an isolated prison camp miles behind the front line, but right in the middle of a defence position that the Japanese soldiers were preparing. There was an atmosphere of acute tension; it was clear that an Allied invasion was expected. Their camp commandant was the one who had cruelly ill-treated them in the previous camp. Every day a number of the prisoners were punished by being staked to the ground in front of the guard-house. The day came, however, when the ground in front of the guard-room was empty. It could only mean one thing—the Japanese were on the point of surrender. This was confirmed later that day. It now became apparent that the spirit of forbearance and love shown to the wounded Japanese soldiers in the railway siding had not been an isolated instance of goodwill. When Allied troops liberated the prison camp they were so infuriated by what they saw that they would have executed the Japanese guards on the spot. It was only the intervention of the prisoners that prevented it.

As the business of repatriation got under way, Ernest made anxious enquiries about the fate of his Chungkai friends, Dinty Moore and Dusty Miller. He learned that Dinty had been designated to go by sea to work in Japan. He and several hundred other prisoners were packed like coal into an ancient hulk which bore no red crosses to show that it was carrying POW's. In consequence, it was torpedoed by an American submarine and sunk. Dennis Moore was one of the many who perished. Eventually Ernest met a prisoner who could tell him what had happened to Dusty Miller. He had been in a gang of prisoners sent to Burma to hack out a retreat route for the Japanese army. The Japanese warrant officer in charge of Dusty's work-party grew to detest him, not because he had done anything wrong, but because he was a *good* man whose spirit could not be broken. Just before the Japanese surrender, this warrant officer, near beserk with hate, had Dinty crucified on a tree. He died, like his Master, condemned by his own goodness.

It was with mixed and poignant memories that Ernest began the journey back to Britain. Fired with idealism as a result of the life-transforming experiences in the prison camps, he came home hoping to find the whole community life of the country transformed by a new spirit—everyone being unselfishly concerned for the welfare of others, just as the camps had come to be. He was soon disillusioned. As their troop-ship sailed up the Mersey, it was learned that the Liverpool dockers were threatening to strike for higher wages. The home-coming prisoners found it difficult to understand why the dockers should refuse to land supplies of food which were urgently needed by the civilian population merely because they wanted higher pay for themselves. A delegation of Scots soldiers approached Ernest requesting him to offer their services to work the docks. Ernest put the proposition to the harbourmaster, who looked at him as though he had gone out of his mind, and then told him that the offer was totally unacceptable as it might precipitate a national dock strike.

Another sickening incident occurred on their arrival in Glasgow. Ernest went into a hotel to cancel a reservation that had been made in his name. The hall porter took one look at his travel-stained pack and kit bag and told him that such filthy luggage could not be left in the hall of a hotel like their's. Ernest realised that 'the day of the soldier was over'.

Acclimatisation to civilian life was a traumatic experience. Like so many other former POW's, Ernest had come home convinced that he had learned lessons important to mankind. He had seen how the love of Christ could work miracles in a prison camp, and he had assumed that it could be even more effective in an environment of freedom. He made the painful discovery that he had returned to a world where there was still hatred and tension, and to a nation where there was irresponsible self-seeking and moral cynicism. He went regularly to church, but even there what he saw and heard depressed him, for it seemed to belong to a bygone age.

Nonetheless, Ernest was determined to keep the resolution he had made to become an ordained minister. The next six years were spent studying theology. He was at a theological college in Edinburgh for two years before going with his wife to Connecticut for a further two years, where he pursued post-graduate studies. He returned to Scotland where he served as assistant minister at Paisley Abbey before going back to America.

Many of those he had seen die in the prison camps had been very young, and Ernest cherished a desire to minister to those of college age. The opportunity came when, in 1955, he was appointed Dean of the Chapel of Princeton University, New Jersey. Here he found young people who shared his dissatisfaction with the materialism that is so chracteristic of modern society; they, at least, seemed eager to search for a deeper meaning to life.

Although life on the university campus was so different from
that of the prison camps, Ernest Gordon found that the questions raised by the students were the same. In the Epilogue of
his book, *Miracles on the River Kwai,* he writes,

> 'The miracle I knew in the jungle was being repeated daily
> on the campus—the miracle of God at work in His world. . .
> In the prison camp we had discovered nothing new. The
> grace we had experienced is the same in every generation
> and must be received afresh in every age. . . . I see that the
> victory over the impersonal, destructive and enslaving
> forces at work in the world has been given to mankind
> because of what Jesus has done. This is the good news for
> man: God, in Christ, has shared his suffering; for that is
> what God is like. He has not shunned the responsibility of
> freedom. He shares the saddest and most painful ex-
> periences of His children, even that experience which
> seems to defeat us all, namely death.
>
> He comes into our Death House to lead us through it.' [6]

References

Grateful acknowledgement is made to the Author and Publisher of 'Miracle on
the River Kwai': Ernest Gordon: Fontana, 1966:

1. p. 95.   2. p. 101.   3. p. 135.   4. p. 150   5. p. 163.
6.. pp. 188, 189.

For Further Reading

'Miracle on the River Kwai': Ernest Gordon: Wm. Collins Sons & Co. Ltd, 1963:
    Fontana Books, 1965

Other similar stories:

'Captives To Freedom': Douglas Thompson: Epworth Press, 1955; Wyvern
    Books, 1965

'John Leonard Wilson—Confessor of the Faith': Roy McKay: Hodder and
    Stoughton Ltd, 1973; Pbk. Ed. 1974

See also under Chapter 4: John Dodd

Film

'Bridge Over the River Kwai': (contains an element of fiction): Columbia
    Warner, 135 Wardour Street, London, W.1.

CHAPTER EIGHT

The Bible Smuggler
Brother Andrew

Born 1928

'Halt!' The German soldier who shouted the command was on
patrol duty in Witte, a small Dutch town which had been
occupied by the German army in May 1940. The soldier was
aware of someone creeping suspiciously along the darkened
street. He shone his torch full on the small figure of Andrew, a
twelve-year-old Dutch boy, who was in fact carrying nothing
more dangerous than a large fire-work. Andrew heard the
ominous 'clack' as the German drew back his rifle-bolt ready to
fire. Hurriedly he lit the fuse, threw the fire-work and then ran
for his life. This was only one of several such foolhardy pranks
by a high-spirited youngster intent on harassing the soldiers
occupying his country.

In the Spring of 1945, Holland was liberated. Andrew was
seventeen years old and now had to decide on a career. He was
still eager for adventure and in January 1946 he joined the
Dutch army; the following November he was posted to In-
donesia. Before his departure, Andrew went home to say
farewell to his girl-friend, Thile, and to his own family. As he
was about to leave, his mother handed him a small Bible.

'Andrew,' she said, 'will you take this with you?'

'Yes, Andrew replied.

'Will you read it, Andrew?' she asked.

Andrew had not the heart to say 'no'. He pushed the little
book to the bottom of his duffle-bag and promptly forgot all
about it.

At first, Andrew enjoyed the Indonesian War; although it was not so much the danger as the killing that excited him. Then, one day an incident occurred which he was never to forget. His unit had been in daily combat for three weeks. They were desperately tired, their nerves on edge. Suddenly, as they marched through a seemingly friendly village, they stepped into a concealed mine-field. The unit went berserk, shooting every living creature within sight. Afterwards, as they walked warily through the devastation they had created, Andrew saw the sight that would always haunt him—a young Indonesian mother lay on the ground, a baby at her breast. Both had been killed by the same bullet—it could have been one of his.

Andrew felt so bitterly ashamed that he wished he could die. In the next two years he courted death by acts of foolhardy bravado. He became famous as the crazy Dutchman who always wore a bright yellow straw hat in combat, as if to invite the enemy to shoot him. One day they did. A bullet smashed his ankle and that, for him, was the end of the Indonesian War.

Andrew lay in hospital, his right leg encased in plaster. He was only twenty years old and yet he felt disgusted with himself and with life. Soon after his admission to hospital, a friend brought in his duffle-bag containing his private possessions. Among them was his mother's parting gift, the little Bible. He had never looked at it, and probably he would have left it unopened now, but for a conversation he had with one of the Franciscan nuns who staffed the hospital. Andrew had asked her how it was that she and the other nursing sisters were always so cheerful.

'Why, Andrew,' she said, 'you ought to know the answer to that—a good Dutch boy like you. It's the love of Christ.' Her eyes sparkled as she spoke.

'But, you're teasing me, aren't you?' she said, touching the little Bible that was lying with his other bits and pieces on the bedside table. 'You've got the answer *right here*.'

Andrew was intrigued and decided that he would start at the beginning and try to read right through the Bible. Although he found it hard to understand, by the time he had reached St

John's Gospel, he knew that he had discovered the source of the faith possessed by the nursing sisters and by the Christians he had known in Witte. But, as yet, that faith was not for him. Soon after his twenty-first birthday, Andrew was sent back to Holland. He returned still burdened with guilt and nursing a hard core of resentment because he did not think that he would ever walk again without the aid of crutches or a stick.

In September 1949, while in the veterans' hospital at Doorn, a very pretty blonde girl came to Andrew's ward to invite the patients to attend an evangelical tent-meeting being held locally. She promised that a bus would be sent to collect them. Andrew and his fellow patients decided to go, partly on account of the girl's charm and partly because it was an excuse for a night out. They took a bottle of spirits and sat at the rear of the tent drinking and making fun of the preacher. Their noisy ribaldry brought the meeting to a premature conclusion. The preacher asked the Choir to sing, and the congregation joined them in the song 'Let My People Go'.

The next day, for some reason he could not understand, Andrew found the words of that closing song going round and round in his head—'Let them go . . . let me go. . . .' He had not looked at his Bible since returning to Holland, but on a sudden impulse, he turned to it again. He read avidly and with new understanding. He also began to attend Church regularly. Not only did he go twice on Sunday, but nearly every night of the week he would be at one religious meeting or another. His family and friends found it hard to understand this sudden enthusiasm for religion.

On a stormy night in the winter of 1950, as he lay in bed, Andrew seemed to hear once more the singing at the tent-meeting, 'Let my people go . . . let *me* go. . . .' He asked himself what was keeping *him* from being freed from the bondage of guilt and despair which had held him for so long. He recalls how, 'all at once, very quietly, I let go of my ego. . . . I turned myself over to God—lock, stock, and adventure. There wasn't much faith in my prayer. I just said, "Lord, if You will show me the way, I will follow You. Amen." ' [1]

Several weeks later, Andrew went with Kees—a boyhood friend—to Amsterdam to hear the Dutch evangelist, Arne Donker. Towards the end of the meeting, Pastor Donker said, 'Friends, I've had the feeling all night that . . . someone out there in the audience wants to give himself to the mission field.' Somewhat reluctantly, Andrew and Kees were persuaded to answer his invitation. The following Saturday afternoon, under the supervision of Pastor Donker, they each gave their testimony at an open-air meeting in the centre of Witte.

The evangelist had advised Andrew to get a job in a local factory and make *that* his first mission-field. So, heeding this advice, Andrew went to work at Ringers' chocolate factory in nearby Alkmaar. There he was instrumental in the conversion of Greetje, a girl who was notorious for her foul talk and the bad influence she had on the other girls. Andrew also discovered that the slender blonde who worked in the time-keeper's office was the same girl who had invited the hospital patients to the tent-meeting. Her name was Corrie van Dam. Andrew was thrilled to find another Christian working there, and they teamed up to help any of the other workers who had personal problems or who simply needed someone to talk to. A prayer group was started in the factory and Greetje put in charge of attendance. She was a natural leader and, together with Andrew and Corrie, shared in the transformation that took place among the workers at Ringers'.

Andrew was promoted and given a more responsible job. Although he enjoyed his new work, he had the feeling that God was calling him to something else. He spent two more years at the factory and during that time he heard about the Worldwide Evangelisation Crusade (WEC), a British based group which trains missionaries to go to those parts of the world where no other Churches are engaged in evangelism. Andrew's friend, Kees, had already decided to become a minister, and when Andrew told him about the WEC he decided to apply for a place at their College in Glasgow; he was accepted immediately.

Andrew, however, had not yet reached the point when he really *knew* what was God's plan for his life. He asked himself:

was the idea of becoming a missionary merely a romantic dream? One Sunday afternoon in September 1952, he went for a walk across the open fields where he could pray aloud without embarrassment. He sat on a canal bank until evening. Gradually, he came to see that he was using his lack of education and his lameness as excuses for not taking the same step as his friend, Kees; he was now ready to say 'Yes' to God.

> 'I'll go, Lord.' He said, 'Whenever, wherever, however You want me, I'll go. And I'll begin this very minute. Lord, as I stand up from this place, and as I take my first step forward, will You consider that this is a step toward complete obedience to You? I'll call it the Step of Yes.'

He stood up and took a stride forward. As he did so, he felt a sharp wrench in his lame leg. To his astonishment he found he could now walk normally and without pain. Surely, he thought, this was a sign sent to confirm the rightness of the decision he had made.

Andrew lost no time in applying for a place at the WEC College. His original girl-friend, Thile, did not want him to become a missionary and they broke off their friendship. In spite of this and a number of other set-backs which delayed his admittance to College, in September 1953 Andrew began his training with the WEC in Glasgow. There, his chief difficulty was to overcome the handicap of language and his lack of formal education. He learned many things, academic and practical, but most important of all, he learned to trust God for all the material needs of life. Although he had no regular source of income, he found that in one way or another, all his financial obligations were met during the two-year course.

Towards the end of his training, in the Spring of 1955, Andrew happened to pick up a magazine from a pile of rubbish and idly scan its contents. It was an act that changed the course of his life. The magazine contained the announcement of a Youth Festival to be held in Warsaw that coming July. He guessed that it was sponsored by the International Socialist Movement, but he applied for a place explaining that he was a student-minister interested in an exchange of ideas. Somewhat to his surprise, he was accepted.

During the tightly programmed visit that followed, Andrew managed to make contact with a number of Polish Christians. He was concerned to know the state of the Church under a Communist regime. At one Church, he was invited to preach, using an interpreter. At the conclusion of his brief address, Andrew was thanked by the pastor. His words made a deep impression. 'We thank you,' he said, *'for being here.* Even if you had not said a word, just seeing you would have meant so much. We feel at times as if we are all alone in our struggle.'

Andrew had brought with him some little booklets of Scriptural quotations in Polish, entitled, *The Way of Salvation.* These he distributed openly at street corners. This attempt to propagate the Christian Gospel seemed insignificant compared with the massive pressure of indoctrination by the Communist regime. On his last day in Warsaw, as he sat praying on a bench by the side of a broad avenue, he heard the sound of martial music. It was the March of Triumph held to conclude the Festival. Hundreds of young Socialists marched by singing. They were possessed by a new 'religion', an ideology that did not include God. In that moment, Andrew *knew* where he was needed as a missionary. It was here, and in the other countries behind the Iron Curtain; it was where the faithful remnant of the Church was struggling for its very survival.

A few weeks later, the leader of the Dutch delegation to the Warsaw Festival invited Andrew to 'represent' the Church on a four-week visit to Czechoslovakia. It was in Prague that he became aware how few people actually possessed Bibles of their own in Communist controlled countries. At the first Church service that he attended there, he noticed how anyone fortunate enough to have a copy held it above his head in order that those worshippers near by could follow the reading. In that moment he realised how much for granted he had taken the possession of a Bible of his own.

Back in Holland, Andrew applied for permission to visit other countries behind the Iron Curtain. At first he was unsuccessful, and so he answered an appeal for volunteers to help in the huge refugee camps which had been established in West Germany following the Hungarian Uprising in 1956. After some months of relief work in the camps, he heard that he had been granted a visa to visit Yugoslavia. About this time, some Christian friends felt led by God to present him with an almost new Volkswagen car. Other friends provided him with money, and Andrew bought up as much Christian literature as he could find printed in the Yugoslavian language. In the Spring of 1957, he set off with tracts, Bibles and portions of Scripture concealed in various places in the Volkswagen.

At that time, the Yugoslav government did not allow visitors to bring in anything except articles for personal use; anything *printed* was particularly liable to confiscation. As Andrew drew near the frontier he prayed, 'Lord, in my luggage I have Scripture that I want to take to Your children across this border. When You were on earth, You made blind eyes see. Now, I pray, make seeing eyes blind. Do not let the guards see those things You do not want them to see.'

At the barrier one of the guards questioned him while the other looked inside the car. Andrew was asked to open his suitcase. The second guard lifted a pile of shirts and, to Andrew's dismay, a bundle of tracts lay revealed. Andrew engaged the first guard in conversation. When he glanced round he found that the other guard was too intent on following the conversation to notice the offending literature.

'Well then, anything else to declare?' he asked.

'Only small things,' Andrew said.

'We won't bother with them,' said the guard. With a silent prayer of gratitude, Andrew closed the suitcase, started the car and proceeded on his way.

His first stop was Zagreb. There, Andrew made contact with Jamiel, a Christian leader who was able to put him in touch with other Yugoslavian Christians. Accompanied by a young engineering student named Nikola, Andrew travelled from place to place preaching and distributing Biblical material—sometimes openly, sometimes secretly.

When they reached Macedonia, another guide, known as 'Little Uncle', came with them. It was at this stage in his tour that Andrew had his first serious encounter with the Yugoslavian police. In one village, a service had been arranged in a private house. Andrew was to have preached, but during the second hymn, there was a loud pounding on the door. When it was opened, two uniformed policemen walked in. They looked carefully at every face in the room and then took down their names. No arrests were made at the time, but Andrew was to hear later that Nikola had been summoned before a court in Zagreb. He was fortunate to be let off with a severe reprimand and a fine. 'Little Uncle', however, was tried and deported.

After this unpleasant incident, Andrew and Nikola travelled on to Belgrade, arriving on May Day. There they had an experience which, Andrew believes, shaped his ministry from that day on. He was preaching to a large congregation and, at the conclusion of his sermon, he invited those present either to commit their lives to Christ or to reaffirm a previous commitment. To his surprise, the entire congregation responded. Andrew began to stress the need for the newly converted to pray and read the Bible regularly. Then he noticed that the people present seemed curiously embarrassed. He turned to the pastor, who explained the reason. 'Prayer, yes,' he said, 'but Bible reading. . . . Brother Andrew, most of these people *do not have Bibles.*'

Andrew turned to the congregation and asked how many of them owned a Bible. Seven hands were raised, including the pastor's. Andrew was stunned. He had given away all the Bibles he had brought, so he helped the pastor to work out a system of Bible-sharing. 'But that same evening,' he recalls, 'a resolve was born in me, a resolve that has burned brighter with each passing year. That night I promised God that as often as I could lay my hands on a Bible, I would bring it to these children of His behind the wall that men had built.' [2]

His visit to Yugoslavia lasted seven weeks. During that time, Andrew travelled nearly six thousand miles, held approximately one hundred meetings and services, witnessed a great many conversions, and established some very useful contacts for any future visit.

However, in spite of such encouraging results, Andrew was conscious of a growing feeling of loneliness. His thoughts often turned to Corrie van Dam. She, in the meantime, had left the chocolate factory and was now a trained nurse. With some difficulty, Andrew eventually tracked her down and asked her to marry him. He left Corrie to consider his proposal while he went off to Hungary, taking with him as many Bibles and tracts in the Hungarian language as he could beg or buy.

On his return, Andrew went direct to Corrie and, to his delight, she agreed to be his wife. They were married on 27 June 1958. Soon afterwards, they set off together to deliver bundles of clothing to the German refugee camps.

Andrew spent the next two weeks travelling through southern East Germany, preaching with surprising freedom to Christians who had plenty of Bibles but who, nonetheless, were more demoralised than any of the other Christian people he had met behind the Iron Curtain. While he was away, Corrie stayed on in West Berlin, using her experience as a nurse to improve the conditions in which the refugees were living.

Next, Andrew made a return visit to Yugoslavia, this time accompanied by his wife. In Zagreb he was met again by Jamiel and Nikola; they were overjoyed to see the recently married couple, and the Bibles that they brought were received with tearful gratitude. Their visit was cut short unexpectedly when, at the end of the first week, they were arrested. The Yugoslavian police were well informed on Andrew's previous visit, and he and Corrie were ordered to leave the country immediately and not return. Andrew's passport was stamped accordingly.

To compensate for this disappointment, when they reached West Berlin again, Andrew was pleased to learn that he had been granted permission to visit Bulgaria and Rumania, two countries where persecution of the Church was particularly intense. He discovered that there were Churches in both countries where there was not even *one* copy of the Bible. The literature which he shared out was deeply appreciated. In some place, however, he would find a pastor and congregation who were too frightened of the secret police to risk accepting any kind of Christian literature.

Andrew arrived home just in time for the birth of a son. In the following twelve months, he revisited every country which would grant him permission to re-enter. Anonymity was becoming a problem, and he stopped using his full name and instead used the name by which he was known by Christians behind the Iron Curtain—'Brother Andrew'. As his work became more widely known, he received offers of help and donations of money from Christians living in many countries of the 'free' world. Somehow, the money that was sent to him always seemed to cover exactly the expenses involved in obtaining his supplies of literature and the cost of his travelling.

In the year that his second son was born, Andrew made his first trip to Russia. It was to accompany a group of young people from Holland, Germany and Denmark to a Youth Congress in Moscow. He went to a Sunday Service at the only Protestant Church still open in Moscow and was amazed to see some two thousand people packed inside a Church built to seat a thousand. Although he was assured that they were not short of Bibles, he had the impression that this was only said to satisfy the authorities. He left with them the three Bibles he had been able to bring to the Congress.

As the work expanded, it became clear that additional help was urgently necessary. Andrew and Corrie prayed for guidance in finding the right person. Soon after, they were joined by Hans, a six-feet-seven Dutchman. One of his first assignments was to accompany Andrew on a return visit to Russia, smuggling in over a hundred Bibles. They linked up with a Russian Christian named Markov, who was willing to distribute them to pastors over as wide an area as possible. Their initial problem was the transfer of the sacks and cartons containing the precious consignment without attracting the attention of the State police. Markov suggested a bold expedient. In a street not two minutes walk from Red Square, Andrew parked his car behind that of Markov. There they did the exchange, on a busy sidewalk, in broad daylight. Andrew and Hans then left Moscow and journeyed home by way of the Ukraine, leaving their one remaining carton of Bibles with the Christians they met there.

During the 1960s, Andrew's unusual type of missionary work continued to develop. Several factors contributed to its extension—the addition of their 'team' of several new helpers; the acquisition of a van built especially for long-distance travel; and the production of *pocket-sized* Bibles in the Slavic language which made it possible to carry a much larger number of copies at a time.

Meanwhile, Andrew had been eager to assess the situation in Communist controlled countries *outside* Eastern Europe. In 1965, he managed to obtain a visa to visit Red China. It was a depressing experience. In Shanghai he found a small store which was well stocked with Bibles, but had pitifully few customers. In several cities he tried to give away Chinese Bibles; time after time they were handed back courteously but with complete indifference as to their contents. Andrew visited six huge communes, none of which had a church. A commune leader told him with obvious pride, 'In the communes, sir, you will find no churches. You see, religion is for the helpless. Here in China we are not helpless any more.' Similar visits by Andrew's co-workers to Cuba and Albania were somewhat frustrating experiences, too. Nonetheless, the opportunities in Europe multiplied, and by the end of the 1960s, there were twelve members of the team all fully occupied.

The situation *today* in the Communist controlled nations is not the same as it was when Andrew began his activities. In Yugoslavia, for instance, Bibles can now be bought openly and possessed legally; yet in some other countries there are more restrictions than ever before. One hopeful sign is the way in which Christians of one Iron Curtain country are now helping those of another. The most encouraging feature of the 1970s, however, is the ever-increasing freedom of travel to Communist states. This has provided the opportunity for tourists who are Christians to act as Bible couriers—simply by taking with them just one copy of a Bible in the appropriate language. This can then be left in any church visited. In this way a considerable number of Bibles can be distributed without undue risk.

Brother Andrew (as he is now known) began his enterprise working, humanly speaking, on his own. His mission has grown internationally under the name of 'Open Doors', the title adopted in 1965 for the organisation which had evolved. Good co-ordination of its various world-wide projects is essential, and an executive Vice-President was appointed in 1975 to facilitate the smooth running of what has now become a large organisation. It has offices in the United States, Canada, New Zealand, South Africa, the Philippines and Switzerland. 'Open Doors' continues to specialise in taking the Christian Gospel by the written and spoken word to those lands where evangelism is officially forbidden.

As to the future—Brother Andrew is particularly concerned to 'open the door' into mainland China. In September 1975 he promoted a Conference, 'Love China '75', which was held in Manila and attended by Chinese Christian leaders and representatives from other countries who are concerned for the survival of the Church in this Republic of nearly 800 million people.

After an initial period of work in and around China, Brother Andrew envisages becoming involved in the Arab and Moslem world. He is well aware of the enormous difficulties he and his fellow missionaries face, but with characteristic faith and hope, he writes: 'It is a tremendous challenge, an impossibly large task, but then we serve the God of the impossible, and nothing is too hard for Him.' [3]

References

Grateful acknowledgement is made to the Authors and Publishers of the literature cited below:

1. 'God's Smuggler': Spire Books, 1968 p. 41.
2. Ibid, p. 108.
3. 'Open Doors Magazine': February/March 1975, p.4.

For Further Reading

'God's Smuggler': Brother Andrew with John and Elizabeth Sherrill: Spire Books, 1968; Hodder and Stoughton, 1968

'Open Doors with Brother Andrew'—International English Language edition; bi-monthly magazine published by Open Doors International Headquarters

For Further Information

Open Doors International Headquarters: P.O. Box 47, Ermelo, Holland

Open Doors (British Office): P.O. Box 6, Standlake, Witney, Oxon OX8 7SH

Audio-Visual Aids

The Church in Eastern Europe: Slide-Sound Presentation. 25 mins. suitable for church meetings and services

Tape Recordings by Brother Andrew and others—full list available

The above may be ordered from Open Doors (British Office).

CHAPTER NINE

Champion of Freedom

Martin Luther King, Jr

Born 1929

'He was the first Negro minister whom I ever heard who can reduce the Negro problem to a spiritual matter and yet inspire the people to seek a solution on this side of Jordan, not in life after death.' These are the words of the Negro author, Louis Loman, describing the man who became known as one of this century's greatest champions of freedom.

Martin Luther King, Jr was born in Atlanta, Georgia, on 15 January 1929, the second of three children. His father was the pastor of the Negro Ebenezer Baptist Church, Atlanta. In his younger days, Martin played happily with the other small children of the neighbourhood. Some, like him, were black, others were white. However, soon after he started school, the parents of his white friends told him not to play any more with their children. When Martin asked why not, one of the parents replied, 'Because we are white and you are coloured.' He ran home in tears to his mother. She took him on her lap and explained how the Negro people had once been slaves and how there were still some white people who thought that they were superior and made laws to keep black and white apart. 'But,' said his mother, 'always remember, you are just as good as anybody else.'

Martin was educated in the segregated public and private schools of Atlanta, entering Morehouse College in 1944, at the age of fifteen. By this time he had resolved to dedicate his life to improving conditions for his people. In his early days at

Morehouse he considered a career as a doctor or lawyer, rather than a Church minister, as his father was.

Martin's parents were reasonably well-off, and he realised that he had led a comparatively sheltered life. He wanted to know at first hand the conditions in which the poorer black people lived and worked. During the long summer vacations he took several jobs which involved hard manual labour. He worked under white bosses and learned what it felt like to be called 'nigger' and to suffer daily humiliations because of his race. He also discovered that there were many *white* people who were treated almost as badly as those who were dark-skinned. He became even more determined to fight for the rights of *all* who were oppressed.

Gradually, Martin came to realise that a Church pastor has unique opportunities of leadership and service in the community, and when he was seventeen he told his father that he felt a call to the ministry. In 1947 he was ordained and became his father's assistant at the Ebenezer Baptist Church.

Martin graduated from Morehouse when he was only nineteen and continued his studies at Crozer Theological Seminary and, later, at Boston University. On 18 June 1953 he married Coretta Scott, a student of music he had met in Boston. In spite of the opportunities that were open to him in the North, Martin was by now convinced that his place was as the pastor of a Negro Church in the Southern States, for it was there that racial discrimination was at its worst. In September 1954, he became minister of the Dexter Avenue Baptist Church in Montgomery, Alabama. In the spring of the following year, the University of Boston awarded him the degree of Ph.D. in Systematic Theology. Martin and his wife were soon fully immersed in the work of the church and community; Martin became known as 'the friendly pastor', and quickly gained a reputation for his powerful preaching.

From the commencement of his ministry, Martin was committed to oppose all forms of racial discrimination. One of the worst forms of racism in Montgomery was segregation on the city buses. Although seventy per cent of Montgomery's bus passengers were black, the first seats on all buses were reserved for whites. If there were not sufficient seats for white passengers, then black people seated in the rear were obliged to give them their seats. There was mounting resentment among the Negro population over such unjust treatment.

On 1 December 1955, an incident occurred which not only brought matters to a head in Montgomery, but also changed the course of Martin's life. A coloured seamstress, Mrs Rosa Parks, was on her way home from work. She took an empty seat in the Negro section of the bus. At the next stop several white people climbed aboard. The driver ordered Mrs Parks to give up her seat to a white man. Rosa was not a defiant type of person, but she was very tired, and so she remained seated. As the bus driver was unable to get her to stand, he called the police, and she was arrested.

News of the arrest soon spread, and the Negro community were enraged. Martin offered his Church for a meeting of black ministers and civic leaders. It was decided to recommend a boycott of the buses until the Negroes were given the same right as the whites to sit where they pleased. The Montgomery Improvement Association was formed to campaign for Negro rights in the community, and Martin was elected its first president.

It was a long and bitter struggle. Many black people were beaten-up and many were arrested. Six weeks after the boycott began, Martin himself was arrested, finger-printed and then released. There were continuous abusive phone calls and threats that he and his wife and their baby would be killed unless the boycott of the buses was called off.

One evening, when Martin was out at a meeting, a bomb was thrown into his house. Although it did considerable damage, his wife and child escaped harm. However, the sound of the explosion was heard all over the neighbourhood and a crowd of Negroes gathered, intent on vengeance. Martin hurried home to find the police holding back a crowd of furious people. Many of them were armed, some with guns, some with broken bottles. It was a critical moment, for this was the first real test of

Martin's Christian principles and of his theory of non-retaliation.

He held up his hand and the crowd fell silent. In a calm voice, he said,

> 'My wife and baby are all right. I want you to go home and put down your weapons. We cannot solve this problem through retaliatory violence. We must meet violence with non-violence. Remember the words of Jesus: "He who lives by the sword will perish by the sword." We must love our white brothers, no matter what they do to us. We must make them know that we love them. Jesus still cries across the centuries, "Love your enemies." This is what we must live by. We must meet hate with love.'

Martin's voice shook with emotion as he concluded,

> 'Remember, if I am stopped, this Movement will not stop, because God is with this Movement. Go home with this glowing faith and this radiant assurance.'[1]

The people dispersed quietly, many of them with tears on their faces. A white policeman was heard to say, 'If it had not been for that nigger preacher, we'd all be dead.'

The boycott lasted over a year; but just before Christmas 1956 the City Council gave in and black people were allowed to sit where they liked on the city's buses. The Revd Dr Martin Luther King, Jr had won his first non-violent victory and, in so doing, he had become a hero to the black people all over the United States.

In 1957, the Southern Christian Leadership Conference (the SCLC) was founded. It fully accepted the policy of non-violence which Martin had come to represent. Its aim was to campaign for 'Civil Rights' for Negroes—the right to live where they liked, to receive proper education, to exercise their vote and to enjoy full citizenship. Martin felt that the Eisenhower Administration was moving too slowly with regard to Negro voting rights and it was decided to organise a 'Prayer Pilgrimage of Freedom' to be held in Washington in May. At noon on 17 May

1957 thirty-seven thousand marchers, including three thousand white sympathisers, assembled at the foot of the Lincoln Memorial. They were addressed by several influential black leaders. Martin gave the closing speech, which was also broadcast on radio. He spoke with moving eloquence. The people of America were left in no doubt that Dr Martin Luther King, Jr had emerged as the nation's supreme champion of Civil Rights.

Although there were no major confrontations during the following year, Martin was very active in his new tasks. He travelled 780,000 miles, delivered two hundred and eight speeches and wrote his first book, *Stride to Freedom*. A few days before it was published in September 1958, Martin was arrested for not obeying a policeman's order to 'move on'. When convicted, he was prepared to go to jail. However, he was released when the Police Commissioner, hoping to save Montgomery's public officials from bad publicity, paid the fine himself. A fortnight later, while Martin was signing copies of his new book in a Harlem store, there was consternation when a Negro woman stabbed him, the knife narrowly missing his heart. There was some suspicion of a possible conspiracy against Martin. It turned out, however, to be only the wild act of a mentally deranged woman. After three weeks in hospital, Martin was discharged. A period of recuperation provided an opportunity to visit India where he met the Prime Minister, Jawaharlal Nehru.

In order to meet the increasing demands of the Civil Rights Movement, Martin moved to Atlanta and once more became assistant pastor to his father at Ebenezer Baptist Church. The year 1960 heralded a new technique of non-violent action—the 'sit-in'. It was first used in North Carolina where students were seeking to desegregate lunch counters and restaurants. Martin accepted an invitation to sit-in at a lunch counter, and as a result, he was arrested together with seventy-five students. Martin was not released when eventually the students were set free. Instead, he was taken in handcuffs to answer a further charge.

Earlier in the year Martin had overlooked the need to change his Alabama driving licence for one issued in Georgia and he had been arrested for driving with an invalid licence. For this offence he had been fined, given a suspended sentence, and released on probation. He was now accused of violating his probation by taking part in the sit-in, and sentenced to six month's hard labour. Meanwhile, Senator John F. Kennedy, who was in the last stage of his campaign for the Presidential election, had heard of Martin's arrest. Mrs Coretta King was astonished to receive a long-distance telephone call from Senator Kennedy promising his help. His intervention was so effective that the next day Martin was released. The election took place a few days later and John F. Kennedy became President of the USA. Many believe that the publicity given to that telephone call to Mrs King won Senator Kennedy his narrow victory. Be that as it may, the new President remained a staunch supporter of Martin and his cause.

The sit-ins continued throughout the Southern states, and as a result, integration was accomplished in hundreds of places. Although not the originator, Martin supported the 'Freedom Rides' that were achieving considerable success in desegregating public transport. The SCLC next campaign was at Albany, Georgia, a totally segregated city. Martin and the Revd Ralph Abernathy (a close friend and the 'second in command' of the SCLC) led a large procession to the City Hall. They were all arrested, but in the negotiations that followed, a degree of desegregation was achieved.

The struggle continued in Albany throughout the summer of 1962. Martin and Ralph were again arrested, this time for taking part in a prayer vigil. The city authorities prevented any further actions of the Civil Rights Movement by obtaining a federal injunction against demonstrations. Martin spent hours trying to decide whether to obey the injunction or not. Many of the leaders, especially the student leaders, felt that the demonstration should go on. Because it was a federal ruling, Martin decided to obey it, although later he regretted his decision, as the impetus of the movement now seemed lost. Furthermore, Martin was criticised by some of his radical followers who felt that more militant action was necessary. The results of the campaign in Albany were not as dramatic as in Montgomery, nevertheless the campaign did give the people of Albany a new sense of dignity and it also helped to clear the way for later reforms in south-west Georgia.

In 1963, the focus of attention for the SCLC was Birmingham, Alabama. The climax came when, on Good Friday, Martin and some of the other leaders defied a court injunction and led a peaceful march to the downtown area of the city. All the marchers, including Martin and Ralph Abernathy, were arrested. But once again President Kennedy intervened and secured their release. This not only enabled them to continue organising the protest, but also drew public attention to their campaign. Many of the protesters, including children and teenagers, were savagely treated by the authorities. However, the protest continued because Martin regarded Birmingham as the 'colossus of segregation' and believed that a victory there would crack the 'whole edifice of discrimination'. This proved correct, for within a few months a thousand cities made concessions to the Civil Rights Movement, and the Negro people began to feel a new confidence in their cause. Moreover, as a result of the Birmingham confrontation, President Kennedy began to prepare his controversial Civil Rights Bill.

Martin and the other leaders of the SCLC now decided to capitalise on the momentum generated by the Birmingham success. A massive march for 'Jobs and Freedom' was planned to take place in Washington on 28 August 1963. A quarter of a million people marched to the Lincoln Memorial, among them some sixty thousand whites. There Martin delivered the famous speech in which he described his dream for America. In it he said,

> 'I have a dream that one day this nation will rise up, live out the true meaning of its creed: We hold these truths as self-evident, that all men are created equal. I have a dream that one day on the red hills of Georgia the sons of former slaves and the sons of former slaveowners will be able to sit down together at the table of brotherhood. I have a dream

that one day even the state of Mississippi, a state swelter-
ing with the heat of oppression, will be transformed into
an oasis of freedom and justice. I have a dream that my four
little children one day will live in a nation where they will
not be judged by the colour of their skin, but by the content
of their character. I have a dream that one day every valley
shall be exalted, every hill and mountain shall be made
low. . . . With this faith we will be able to work together, to
pray together, to struggle together, to go to jail together,
to stand up for freedom together, knowing that we will be
free one day. . . . When we allow freedom to ring from
every town and every hamlet, from every state and every
city, we will be able to speed up that day when all of God's
children, black men and white men, Jews and Gentiles,
Protestants and Catholics, will be able to join hands and
sing the words of the old Negro spiritual, "Free at last!
Free at last! Thank God A'mighty, we are free at last!" ' [2]

As Martin ended, there was an awed silence and then an
ecstatic roar as the crowd re-echoed and applauded his words.

The march on Washington had immediate results. President
Kennedy received the leaders of the Civil Rights Movement at
the White House and later he presented the Civil Rights Bill
to Congress. The main purpose of this measure was to put a
stop to segregation and discrimination, especially in the
Southern States. John F. Kennedy did not live to see his Bill
passed. On 22 November 1963 he was assassinated at Dallas in
Texas. Martin felt the tragedy deeply, and prophesied, 'This is
what is going to happen to me also.' The task which Kennedy
began was continued by President Johnson, and the Bill was
sanctioned by Congress on 2 July 1974. Martin was presented
with the pen with which the President had signed the Bill.

This important step forward had been achieved by non-
violent means, and it earned worldwide admiration. This was
expressed by the award of the Nobel Peace Prize to Martin. He
received it from King Olav V of Norway in Oslo on 10 December
1964. In his speech of acceptance, Martin said,

'Therefore I must ask why this prize is awarded to a Movement which is beleaguered and committed to unrelenting struggle; to a Movement which has not won the very peace and brotherhood which is the essence of the Nobel Prize. After contemplation I conclude that this award which I receive on behalf of the Movement, is a profound recognition that non-violence is the answer to the crucial political and racial questions of our time—the need for man to overcome oppression without resorting to violence.'[3]

He also said,

'I feel as though this prize has been given to me for something that has not yet been achieved. It is a commission to go out and work even harder for the things in which we believe.'

Soon after New Year's Day 1965, Martin went to Selma, in the heart of the black-belt of Alabama. The new campaign was to centre around voting rights for Negroes. While he was busy making preparations, Martin was struck on the head by a white assailant, fortunately escaping serious injury. However, a few days later, in neighbouring Marion, a protest march was broken up and several of the demonstrators were clubbed; one young man was shot dead. In February, Martin and his co-leader, Ralph Abernathy, were arrested again and spent five days in jail. In March a large crowd of demonstrators set off to march from Selma to Montgomery. They were ordered to halt and turn back. As the marchers stood in silence, sixty state troopers charged the defenceless column hitting out with bullwhips and clubs at men, women and children. The wild mélée was seen on television, and the whole nation was shocked at the brutal attack in which more than sixty people were injured. After more demonstrations and further bloodshed, President Johnson spoke out before a joint Congressional session and promised to give priority to his proposed legislation to a Bill entitling Negroes the freedom to use their vote.

The Voting Rights Bill was signed on 6 August 1965, and

represented a major advance in the legal protection of Negro rights. Martin now proposed that the SCLC should expand its activities into the North and West; 'I tell you,' he said, 'we will take the non-violent movement all over the United States.' Martin felt that the tensions in Chicago were so serious that he must first concentrate his attention there in the hope of preventing the eruption of violence. In January 1966, he moved to Chicago to lay the groundwork for the campaign. Coretta and their four children went with him. Martin decided not to stay at a hotel, but to rent a slum apartment in order to share the kind of ghetto life that was imposed on so many of his people.

On 10 July, fifty thousand people took part in a massive rally and demonstration. Mrs King and all four children were on the platform from which the speeches were made, and Martin allowed them to be with him at the head of the enormous crowd which marched on the City Hall when the speeches were over. The Mayor was not available to receive the deputation, so Martin nailed their demands to the closed door of the City Hall. It had been a very effective peaceful demonstration, but the next day some of the Movement's followers were involved in rioting. They were mostly young folk, and Martin and his staff did their best to restrain them. Martin had no hesitation in condemning their behaviour, although he tried to let them see that he understood the frustration they felt; he described rioting as 'the language of the unheard'.

Martin had always had a deep concern for *world* peace, and during 1967 he was particularly outspoken in his condemnation of the war in Vietnam. To him the campaign in the USA for civil rights and freedom for the oppressed was inextricably linked with the crusade for international peace. Back in 1965, he had said, 'It is worthless to talk about integration if there is no world to integrate.' His action brought criticism from some of the other black leaders, who thought that he should concentrate his energies on improving conditions for the Negro. However, as the peace movement was largely composed of whites, Martin saw that this was a unique opportunity for blacks and whites to work together for a common goal. He took part in several mass demonstrations, himself leading the great Spring Mobilisation for Peace held in New York in April 1967. Undoubtedly the stand he took was one of the major factors in influencing the general public to demand the withdrawal of the American military presence in Vietnam.

Early in 1967, Martin decided that the time was ripe to use non-violent pressure to bring about some improvement of the wretched *economic* conditions in which so many people lived, both black and white. Consequently, the Poor People's Campaign was born. Martin described its objectives as: 'Economic security, decent sanitary housing, and quality education for every American.' He travelled from city to city in an endeavour to mobilise the nation to fight poverty of every kind.

He was equally concerned for the poor and hungry in the underdeveloped countries of the world. In a moving speech he said,

'You may not realise how many poor people there are in our world. There are millions of people still going to bed hungry tonight all over the world. I've been to India—on those dark and lonely nights I've seen with my own eyes thousands of people sleeping on the sidewalks. . . . Almost two-thirds of the people of the world are hungry, and have never seen a doctor or dentist. . . . I'm concerned about this.'

Although Martin's speeches and sermons were usually reported fully by the news media, he reached a still wider public through the books he wrote: *Strength to Love* published in 1963, *Why We Can't Wait* in 1964, *Where Do We Go From Here: Chaos or Community?* in 1967 and *The Trumpet of Conscience* in 1968.

The planning of the Poor People's Campaign in 1968, plus the other duties entailed by the SCLC's expanding programme, put a heavy strain on Martin. Moreover, the bitter opposition to him and to his policies was intensified, and both he and his wife had a sense of 'fate closing in'. Martin was aware that his own life was constantly in danger, but this did not deter him from his purpose. In his sermons he often said, 'If a man has not found something worth giving his life for, he is not fit to live.' He was also heard to say, 'I may be crucified for my beliefs, and if I am, you can say, "He died to make men free." '

In April 1968 Martin was in Memphis, Tennessee, leading a campaign in support of a demand by the garbage workers for better conditions of work. Once again there was a regretful outbreak of violence involving some of his own followers. This greatly depressed Martin and his deep unhappiness was obvious at a press conference he gave following these incidents. However, the next morning he called a second press conference and this time seemed so full of fire that one of the reporters asked him, 'Dr King, what has happened to you since last night? Have you talked with someone?' Martin replied, 'No. I haven't talked with anyone. I have only talked with God.'

A large-scale march was planned to proceed from Memphis to Washington. On Wednesday evening, 3 April Martin received an unexpected phone call to go and address a meeting of about two thousand people. Completely spontaneous, and speaking with great emotion, he gave one of his greatest speeches. He referred to the threats and rumours of an attack on him, and went of to say,

> 'Like anybody else, I would like to live a long life. Longevity has its place. But I'm not concerned about that now. I just want to do God's will. And He's allowed me to go up to the mountain. And I've looked over, and I've seen the Promised Land. I may not get there with you, but I want you to know tonight that we as a people will get to the Promised Land. So I'm happy tonight. I'm not worried about anything. I'm not fearing any man. Mine eyes have seen the glory of the coming of the Lord. . .' [4]

So intense was the audience's response that Martin was overcome with emotion and broke off without completing the quotation—'His truth is marching on.'

Martin and his staff were staying at a down-town Negro-owned Motel. On Thursday, 4 April the day following his speech, Martin dressed for dinner and then went out on to a little balcony overlooking the street. He stood breathing in the evening air. Standing below the balcony was Ben Branch, who was to sing at the meeting later in the evening. Leaning over the green railing, Martin called down to him, 'Be sure to sing, "Precious Lord, Take my Hand" for me, tonight, Ben. Sing it real pretty.' They were his last words. A single shot rang out. It sounded no louder than a fire-cracker, but Martin Luther King, Jr slumped down on the concrete floor, fatally wounded.

He was only thirty-nine years old, yet in a few years he had awakened the conscience of a nation to the needs of the under-privileged and poor. He had led Black America towards freedom by giving them *hope*. Above all, he had tried to follow the teaching of Jesus Christ. A tape-recording was played at the funeral service held at Ebenezer Baptist Church. It was part of the last sermon he had preached there. Anticipating his death, Dr King had said,

> 'I'd like someone to mention that day, that. . . "Martin Luther King, Jr, tried to give his life serving others". I'd like for somebody to say that day, that. . . "Martin Luther King, Jr, tried to love somebody" . . . that "I tried to be right on the war question" . . . that "I did try to feed the hungry" . . . that 'I did try, in my life, to clothe those who were naked" . . . that 'I did try, in my life, to visit those who were in prison". I was to say that, ". . . I tried to love and serve humanity." '

The powerful voice filled the church again, the biblical cadences rolling over the tight-packed congregation,

> 'Yes, if you want to say that I was a drum major, say that I was a drum major for justice; say that I was a drum major for peace; I was a drum major for righteousness. And all the other shallow things will not matter. I won't have any money to leave behind. I won't have the fine and luxurious things of life to leave behind. But I just want to leave a committed life behind.

And that's all I want to say . . . if I can help somebody as
I pass along, if I can cheer somebody with a word or song,
if I can show somebody he's travelling wrong, then my
living will not be in vain. If I can do my duty as a Christian
ought, if I can bring salvation to a world once wrought, if I
can spread the message as the master taught, then my
living will not be in vain.' [5]

Martin had always been ready to give his life for the cause in
which he believed. His assassination drew world-wide attention
to the principles for which he stood, and in the days following
his death probably more people heard his message than in the
twelve years he had been preaching.

Although the Bill for Civil Rights had become law, the task to
which Martin had committed himself was an unfinished task, as
Dr Benjamin Mays emphasised at the public service held at
Martin's former College. The President Emeritus of Morehouse
said,

'Let us see to it that he did not die in vain; let us see to it
that we do not dishonour his name by trying to solve our
problems through rioting in the streets. . . . But let us see
to it that the conditions that cause rioting are promptly
removed. . . . Let black and white alike search their hearts;
and if there be any prejudices in our hearts against racial or
ethnic group, let us exterminate it and let us pray, as
Martin Luther King, Jr, would pray if he could: "Father,
forgive them for they know not what they do.'' If we do
this, Martin Luther King, Jr will have died a redemptive
death from which all mankind will benefit.' Dr. Mays
concluded his eulogy, 'I close by saying to you what Martin
Luther King, Jr, believed, that *if physical death was the
price he had to pay to rid America of prejudice and in-
justice, nothing could be more redemptive.* To paraphrase
the words of the immortal John Fitzgerald Kennedy,
permit me to say that Martin Luther King, Jr's unfinished
work on earth must truly be our own.' [6]

Martin Luther King, Jr, is buried in South View Cemetery, Atlanta. On his tomb are carved the triumphant words with which he ended his great speech in Washington in August 1963:

> FREE AT LAST, FREE AT LAST
> THANK GOD ALMIGHTY
> I'M FREE AT LAST

References

Grateful acknowledgement is made to the Author and Publisher of 'My Life With Martin Luther King, Jr': Coretta Scott King: first published by Holt, Rinehart and Wilson, 1969; references below refer to Pbk. Ed.: Hodder and Stoughton Ltd, 1973.

1. p. 143   2. p. 253f.   3. p. 26.   4. p. 328.
5. p. 361.   6. p. 371.

For Further Reading

Books about Martin Luther King, Jr

'Crusader Without Violence': Lawrence Reddick: New York: Harper, 1959

'Martin Luther King, Jr: His Life, Martyrdom and Meaning for the World': William R. Miller: New York: Weybright and Talley, 1968

'Martin Luther King—A Drum Major for Justice': Paul P. Piech: Taurus Press of Willow Dene, 1968

'My Life With Martin Luther King, Jr': Coretta Scott King: New York: Holt, Rinehart and Winston, 1969; London: Hodder and Stoughton Ltd 1970

'What Manner of Man': Lerone Bennett: Chicago: Johnson Publishing Co. 3rd Rev. Ed. 1969; London: Allen and Unwin, 1969

'King—A Critical Biography': David L. Lewis: New York: Praeger, 1970; London: A. Lane, 1970

'Martin Luther King': Kenneth Slack: Centrebooks: SCM Press Ltd, 1970

'We Will Suffer and Die If We Have To'—A Folk Play for Martin Luther King: Colin Hodgetts: REP, 1969

Books by Martin Luther King, Jr

'Stride Toward Freedom'—The Montgomery Story: New York: Harper, 1958; London: Gollancz, 1959

'Strength To Love': New York: Harper, 1963; London: Hodder and Stoughton Ltd, 1964; Fontana, 1969

'Why We Can't Wait': New York: Harper 1964; Signet Books, 1964

'Where Do We Go from Here—Chaos or Community?': New York: Harper, 1967; London: Penguin 1969

'The Trumpet of Conscience': New York; Harper, 1968; London: Hodder and Stoughton Ltd, 1968

'Words and Wisdom—Political Speeches': Taurus Press of Willow Dene, 1970.

Films

'I Have A Dream—The Life of Martin Luther King, Jr': USA 1971. B/w. 35 mins Concord Films Council, Nacton, Ipswich, Suffolk, IP10 0JZ

'Legacy of a Dream': a retrospective view of the civil rights movement of the sixties, showing the growing political power of the black community, and concludes with the 'I have a dream' speech. Col. 29 mins. Concord Films Council.

'Walk To Freedom': the Montgomery bus boycott; non-violent direct action by Negroes in the USA linked with similar action in other countries. B/w. 20 mins. Concord Films Council

'King—Montgomery to Memphis': BBC TV. B/w. 3 hrs. International Personnel, 154 Balham High Road, London SW12 9BN

Filmstrip and Filmslides

'The Dream of Martin Luther King': examines the history and background to the racial problem in the USA. B/w filmstrip with notes and recorded commentary, including extracts from the speech, 'I have a dream': available on reel or cassette; or filmstrip and printed commentary only, from: Carwal—Audio-Visual-Aids Ltd, P.O. Box 55, Wallington, Surrey

'Street Scene—The Negro and Civil Rights in the USA': from the days of the slave trade to the Civil Rights Movement of Martin Luther King: 12 slides: Ref. S614: The Slide Centre Ltd, 143 Chatham Road, London, SW11 6SR

Recordings

'Martin Luther King—Extracts from Speeches and Sermons': Mercury: 20119 SMCL

'Dr Martin Luther King Jr. In the Struggle for Freedom and Human Dignity'—extracts from speeches and sermons: Hallmark CHM 631

CHAPTER TEN

Leader of The Gang

Nicky Cruz

Born 1938

The Mau Maus were one of New York's most vicious gangs. To join them it was necessary to undergo a brutal initiation test; Nicky Cruz stood waiting for his. The first blow hit him in the back, the next in the stomach and the third in the face. He heard the bone of his nose crack under the impact of a clenched fist. With five of the gang's toughest boys hitting him from all angles he had no chance to defend himself. He fell to the floor where he was kicked repeatedly in the body and head. When he regained consciousness, he found himself lying on his back in a pool of blood. His eyes focused on a face peering down at him. The next moment he was lashing out with fists and feet at everyone in sight. Eventually, he was pinned to the ground. Israel, the vice-president of the gang, bent over him, laughing, 'You're our kind, Nick. Man we can use you. You may be a lot of things, but you're not chicken'. As Nicky climbed unsteadily to his feet, Israel pressed something hard into his hand. It was a .32 revolver. 'You're a Mau Mau, Nicky. A Mau Mau,' he said.

Nicky Cruz was just sixteen when he joined the gang. He had been born in Puerto Rico on 12 June 1938, one of a family of seventeen boys and one girl. His parents were spiritualists and earned a living conducting seances and practising sorcery and voodoo. Nicky had an unhappy childhood. He was terrified of the sorcery that took place each night and resented the fact that his parents had so little time for him. When he was eight years old, he walked into a room where his mother was entertaining some other spiritualist mediums. Without any warning, Mrs Cruz went into a trance and began to chant, 'This ... not ... my ... son. No, not Nicky. He never been mine. He child of greatest of all witches, Lucifer. . . . No, not mine. . . . Son of Satan, child of Devil.' Turning on Nicky she shrieked, 'Get out, Devil. Get away from me. . . . Away! Away! Away!' Shaking with fear, Nicky ran to his room. Only one thought spun round in his mind: 'No-one loves me. No-one cares.' He was filled with hate and rage.

During the next five years Nicky became a rebel both at school and at home. He ran away from home five times in two years, and eventually his parents asked Frank, his eldest brother, if Nicky could live with him in New York. Frank agreed and enrolled Nicky at a school in Brooklyn attended mainly by Negroes and Puerto Ricans. It was here that he first encountered the teenage gangs which rivalled each other in school and outside. There was constant fighting, and Nicky was beaten up several times before he learned to defend himself by using the same dirty tactics as the others used. Following a class-room incident in which Nicky hit another boy over the head with a chair, he was expelled from school. He had been there only two months.

Nicky decided to leave Frank and fend for himself. He found a tenement room at Fort Greene Place, Brooklyn, but had no money for the rent. Taking his switchblade knife he went out on the streets and waited in an alley for someone he could rob. A boy in his late teens came by, Nicky pulled him into the alley, held the knife in front of his face and demanded his money. The terrified boy handed over his wallet and ran for his life. Nicky returned to Fort Greene Place and rented the room. He was on his own now—but it felt good.

The next day, Nicky made a tour of the neighbourhood. It proved to be a concrete jungle of drab apartments. In the days that followed, Nicky learned that for his own safety he needed to belong to one of the local gangs. He met a boy who introduced him to Carlos, the president of the Mau Muas, and so it came about that having passed his initiation test he became a member of a gang that even the police feared.

Three nights later he took part in a fight with the Bishops, a rival gang. Armed with knives, pistols, sawn-off shot-guns, bayonets, broken bottles, and baseball bats, the two gangs met in a school playground. About two hundred boys were involved in a vicious battle. As the Bishops retreated, Nicky had his first chance to use his revolver. A small boy who had been hurt was half-running, half-limping behind the fleeing gang. Nicky aimed his gun and pulled the trigger twice. The boy fell, hit in the hip. At that moment the police arrived and the Mau Maus fled, too. Nicky felt elated. He had shot someone, possibly killed him. He was one of the gang. He had never sensed this feeling of belonging before and he recalls, 'It was almost as if we were a family and for the first time in my life I felt like I was wanted.'

Two months later, Carlos, the leader of the Mau Maus was sent to prison and his second-in-command, Israel (now a close friend of Nicky), became president. Nicky was the unanimous choice for vice-president. The next four months were filled with fights, robberies and a variety of crime. On four occasions Nicky was arrested but then released because there was insufficient evidence to convict him. One afternoon he heard that a member of the Apache gang had 'roughed-up' Lydia, his girl-friend. Accompanied by Israel and six of the gang, Nicky found the Apache, knocked him to the ground and then he hit him again and again with a metal pipe until he lay unconscious in a pool of blood. This kind of incident enhanced his reputation as a blood-thirsty hoodlum, and when Israel relinquished the presidency of the Mau Maus, Nicky was his natural successor.

However, unknown to those who imagined him utterly fearless, Nicky was increasingly possessed by guilt and apprehension. For more than two years he dreaded sleeping because of horrific recurrent nightmares. Without the gang—now numbering two hundred boys and seventy-five girls—he believed he would go insane. He did no work, the gang supported him from the proceeds of their nightly robberies. To the Mau Maus he was a hero, to the police the most dangerous gang leader in Brooklyn, but to himself a teenager haunted by demons and desperately afraid of death.

In two years with the Mau Maus Nicky was arrested twenty times. He was only eighteen years old when he appeared in court following his twenty-first arrest. The police described him as a 'mad dog' who needed to be penned up. The judge referred him to the court psychiatrist to determine whether he was psychotic. The psychiatrist took Nicky by car out of the city and into the country. At the end of a whole day together, the doctor told Nicky he was not going to recommend jail because he did not consider it would do him any good. 'Nicky,' he said, 'I'll give it to you straight. You're doomed. There's no hope for you. And unless you change you're on a one-way street to jail, the electric chair, and hell.' Nicky returned to his dingy apartment shaken to the core. He could think of only one thing, 'It's useless. I'm doomed.' He remembered something the judge had said, 'Obviously you don't have anyone to love you—and you don't love anyone either. You don't have the capacity to love. You're sick, Nicky.' He knew he was sick; he had never known real love; he needed love, but where was it to be found?

On a hot Friday afternoon in July 1958, Israel and Lydia were sitting with Nicky on the front steps of his apartment, when they noticed some youngsters running down the street. Hoping for some new excitement, they followed and joined the crowd which was gathering outside a local school. As they elbowed their way to the front, they saw a skinny, weak-looking man standing with his head bowed, a black book open in his hands. The crowd fell strangely quiet. The skinny man looked up and began to read from the black book: ' "God so loved the world that He gave His only begotten son, that whosoever believeth in Him, should not perish, but have everlasting life." ' Nicky felt a cold chill of fear creep up his spine. It was the terror he had felt after the day spent with the psychiatrist—whose words came back to him again, 'Nicky, you're doomed.' The man with the book said he wanted to talk to the leaders of the gangs. 'If you're so big and tough, you wouldn't be afraid of coming up here and shaking hands with a skinny preacher, would you?' The president and vice-president of the Chaplains went forward followed by two

Negro members of their gang. They shook hands and then, to Nicky's amazement, took off their hats and knelt down in the street. Someone yelled, 'Hey, Nicky, you gonna let those niggers show you up? You afraid to go up, too?' Israel beckoned to Nicky, 'Come on, let's go,' he said and pulled him forward. The skinny man walked over to Nicky and offered his hand. 'Nicky,' he said, 'my name is David Wilkerson, 'I'm a preacher from Pennsylvania.' Nicky stared at him and said, 'Go to hell, preacher.' The preacher did not flinch. 'You don't like me, Nicky,' he said, 'but I feel different about you. I love you. And not only that, I've come to tell you about Jesus who loves you, too.' 'You come near me, Preacher and I'll kill you,' Nicky said, and then turned his back on him and barged his way through the crowd.

Later in the evening, Nicky sat in the gang's filthy basement room, drinking and chain smoking, trying desperately to forget those words, 'Jesus loves you'. Suddenly, in walked Wilkerson. He stuck out his hand again. Nicky slapped him hard in the face and spat on him. 'Get the hell out of here!' he yelled and pushed him backwards towards the door. 'I'll give you twenty-four hours to get off my turf or I'll kill you,' he screamed. At the door, Wilkerson still smiling, said, 'Remember, Nicky, Jesus loves you.'

That night Nicky could not sleep. He rose at 5 a.m. and went down to the street. A car pulled up, and there was the preacher again. 'Nicky, you didn't sleep much last night, did you?' he said. 'I didn't either. I stayed awake praying for you. . . . One day, soon, Nicky, God's Spirit is going to deal with you . . . you're going to stop running away and come running to Him.' Nicky turned from him in disgust; but try as he might, he could not rid his mind of Wilkerson's words.

During the second week of July 1958, David Wilkerson issued a personal invitation to all the gangs to come to the closing rally of a Crusade he had been leading. To ensure that the Mau Maus would attend, he reserved seats for them at the front of the auditorium and sent a coach to collect them. Much against his will, Nicky was persuaded to go. The arena was filled to capacity, many of the gangs were there and the noise was deafening. A young girl came out on the stage to sing a gospel song, but her words were drowned by the din. Then Wilkerson appeared and began to speak: 'This is the last night of our city-wide youth crusade. Tonight, we're going to do something different. I'm going to ask my friends, the Mau Maus, to receive the offering.' There was pandemonium, for everyone knew the gang's reputation. Nicky saw this as his chance to get even with the preacher and score a big success with the crowd. Nicky, Israel and four of the Mau Maus walked forward and Wilkerson gave each of them a large ice-cream carton. No-one dared refuse to give and consequently the offering was large. Nicky led the five Mau Maus out through a curtained exit by the side of the stage. All they had to do now was to make off with the money. The others could not believe their ears when Nicky shook his head and said, 'Come on. Let's take this loot to the skinny priest.' To the surprise of the crowd the six of them re-appeared on the stage. Wilkerson took the cartons, looked Nicky straight in the eyes and said, 'Thank you, Nicky. I knew I could count on you.' Then he began to preach. Nicky hardly heard a word, he was only aware of the warm feeling he had experienced as he handed over the collection. For the first time in his life he had done right because he wanted to.

During his address, Wilkerson was interrupted by an outbreak of shouting from the crowd. Israel told the youngsters to quieten down and the preacher continued. Nicky, however, was lost in thought. Scenes from the past seemed to flash before him as if on a cinema screen. He visualised the stabbings, the brutality, the lust, the destruction, the drugs and the drink, and he was overwhelmed with feelings of guilt and shame. Abruptly, Wilkerson's raised voice brought him back to the present. He heard him say, 'Jesus is in this room. He's come especially for you. If you want to have your life changed, now is the time. Stand up and come forward!' Israel did not hesitate, 'Boys, I'm going up. Who's with me?' Nicky stood up, turned to the gang and said, 'Let's go!' At least twenty-five of the Mau Maus responded, followed by about thirty boys from the other gangs. In the counselling room Nicky and Israel knelt side by side laughing and crying. Nicky recalls that moment as the turning-point of his life: 'I opened my mouth but the words that came out were not mine. "O God, if you love me, come into my life. I'm tired of running. Come into my life and change me. Please change me." ' Suddenly a feeling of release and joy swept over him, at the same time his fear and anxiety vanished. Than night, for the first time he could remember, he slept peacefully. No nightmares disturbed nine hours of unbroken sleep.

The next morning, at the local police station, the Desk Sergeant was horrified to see a group of Mau Maus, armed to the teeth, burst through the doors. He reached for his gun. 'Hey, easy man,' Israel said. 'We ain't come to cause no trouble. We've all given our hearts to God and now we want to give our guns to the police.' They piled their fire-arms on the counter, while the police looked on in utter amazement.

Some weeks later, Nicky attended his first Church service. He and Israel told the congregation how their lives had been changed. Afterwards, as Nicky stood outside the church, a fusillade of shots rang out and a hail of bullets smacked into the wall behind him. It was the first of two attempts that night to kill him. On his way home an Apache came at him with a knife. Nicky warded off the blow with his right hand and the knife narrowly missed his chest; his hand was badly gashed and, as a result, he spent two days in hospital. Nicky began to realise the price he might have to pay for becoming a Christian.

Nicky could not forget the feeling of the power and presence of God which he had experienced while he was giving his testimony in church. He began to wonder if God might be wanting *him* to be a preacher. He was invited to give his testimony at another Church and, after he had spoken, many members of the congregation answered the invitation to give their lives to Christ. The feeling that God was calling him to a special ministry grew stronger as he became convinced that God was actually at work in his life. He had a long talk with David Wilkerson, who asked him if he was serious about going into the ministry. Nicky told him that he did not know anything about the ministry nor could he speak intelligible English, but nonetheless, he felt God was leading him in that direction. Wilkerson agreed with him and said that he would try to arrange for Nicky to go to a Bible school.

Two weeks later Nicky was enrolled at The Bible Institute in La Puente, California. The disciplined life of the college was so different from anything Nicky had ever experienced that he found great difficulty in adjusting to it. There was virtually no free time, talking with girl students was forbidden and the lectures were hard for him to understand. In despair, he wrote to Wilkerson asking for a plane ticket back to New York. The reply arrived a week later:

'Dear Nicky,

Glad to hear you are doing so well. Love God and flee Satan. Sorry we have no money in the budget right now. . .

Your friend, David.'

Nicky continued to feel depressed and frustrated. He felt out of place among the other students—'a gangster among saints'. The Dean of the College tried to re-assure him.

'The world needs your voice, Nicky. There are hundreds of thousands of young people all over America who still live as you lived. . . . They will not hear the professional evangelists. . . . They need a prophet out of their own ranks, Nicky. . . . God has touched your life and called you out of the gutter so you may call others to follow in the way of the Cross.'

Everyone at the College told Nicky that his life would change when he was 'baptised by the Holy Spirit'. He prayed more urgently, 'God, it's me, Nicky! I'm here, too. Baptise me!' At first nothing happened and then, one night, after he had finally decided to quit the college, he was conscious of his life being filled with God's Spirit. Nicky describes the change that came over him:

'The days that followed were filled with joy and victory. The first change I noticed was in my conduct . . . I stood at attention during the prayers, praying with the leader. Instead of acting smart I began to show consideration for others, especially the girl who sat in front of me with the beautiful dark eyes.'

Her name was Gloria, and in spite of the strict College rules concerning fraternisation, a romance had already begun to evolve between them.

Towards the end of his second year at the Bible Institute, Nicky received a letter from David Wilkerson asking him to return to New York for the summer vacation to work with the Brooklyn gangs. Nicky jumped at the opportunity. But the day he arrived back in the city he was deeply distressed to hear that his friend, Israel, had slipped back into his old ways. Through an unfortunate misunderstanding, Israel had returned to the gang and had been involved with some other boys in a murder. He had been sentenced to five years imprisonment.

The next day, Nicky set out to look for any members of his former gang who were still in the area. He soon spotted a group of Mau Maus, easily identifiable by the large double 'M' on the back of their jackets. He only recognised one of them, a boy named Willie Cortez. Willie stared at him in disbelief. 'Don't tell me you Nicky? Man, you look like a saint or something,' he said. Nicky took Willie by the arm and walked with him through the park. He told him how God had changed his life and how God could change Willie's, too. There, in the park, they knelt down. Nicky put his hands on Willie's head and began to pray. He felt the boy's body shaking and heard him sobbing, and then Willie began to pray, urgently: 'Jesus, help me! help me!' They remained in the park for the rest of the afternoon. At dusk, Willie set off back to his apartment, promising to bring the rest of the gang to meet Nicky the following night.

Nicky spent that summer with the gang, preaching in the streets and counselling individual members. Before leaving New York he persuaded the Mau Maus to attend a big youth rally. More than eighty-five came. At the close of the service Nicky was asked to speak. He preached for forty-five minutes, pouring his heart out. The tears were streaming down his cheeks as he pleaded with the boys to commit their lives to God. Thirteen of them came forward and knelt at the altar rail.

That summer vacation spent in his old haunts in New York transformed Nicky's whole outlook on life. He returned to the Bible Institute more determined than ever to become a full-time preacher. He now got on well with all the other students, but particularly with Gloria, with whom he was now deeply in love. In the Spring of his final year, Nicky heard from David Wilkerson that he was buying a large old house in Brooklyn to open as a centre for teenagers and drug addicts. It was to be known as Teen Challenge. He invited Nicky to help staff it. The following November, Nicky and Gloria were married, and a month later, began work together at the old three-storey mansion on Clinton Avenue on which Teen Challenge was based.

It soon became clear that their main work was going to be with drug addicts. Many of the youngsters who, previously, had been satisfied to smoke marijuana and drink wine, had now gone on to heroin. The tactic used by Nicky and his associates was to walk up to the groups of boys and girls they found standing on the street corners and say, 'Hey, baby, you want to kick your habit?' Almost invariably they would reply, 'Yeah, man, but how?' They would then be given a tract and invited back to the centre. At first only a few came and it was slow work gaining their confidence. In fact, it was not until May that Nicky had his first success with an addict. The cure involved ceaseless vigilance and inexhaustible patience, but the boy concerned not only overcame his drug-dependence, but also became a Christian. To Nicky and Gloria this made the long hours spent with him abundantly worthwhile.

Most of their work outside the centre was done in open-air meetings and in personal encounters on the streets. Spanish Harlem was the area in which the largest crowds would gather. On one occasion, Mario, a converted gang member, attracted approximately three hundred youngsters simply by going round the streets announcing that: 'The leader of the vicious Mau Maus gang from Brooklyn is going to speak in fifteen minutes— come prepared. He's a killer and still dangerous!' About two hundred adults gathered at the back of the crowd to see what was going on. Two police cars drew up and were stationed on each side of the excited mob. Nicky stood up to speak and was greeted with thunderous applause.

> 'This afternoon,' he began, 'I want to tell you why I'm the *ex*-leader of the Mau-Maus. I'm the *ex*-leader because Jesus changed my heart! One day in a street meeting just like this, I listened to a preacher tell me of someone who could change my life. He told me Jesus loves me. I didn't even know who Jesus was. And I knew *no*body loved me. But Davie Wilkerson told me Jesus loved me. . . . I gave myself to God and He gave me new life. I used to be just like you. . . . But then Jesus changed my life. He gave me something to live for. He gave me hope. He gave me a new purpose in life. . . .'

The crowd was very quiet as Nicky invited them to surrender their lives to Christ. Twenty-two responded and knelt down in the street while Nicky prayed for them. When he finished and looked up he saw that even the police were standing with their hats off and their heads bowed.

In spite of such initial successes, Nicky began to encounter problems which he felt ill-equipped to handle. Forty drug addicts under one roof, supervised by an inexperienced staff, inevitably led to an explosive situation. David Wilkerson was too much occupied with speaking engagements and fund raising for the Centre to be able to spend much time there himself. Nicky was working all hours of the day and night, leaving Gloria very much on her own. The birth of a daughter in January 1963 only partially relieved her loneliness. Nonetheless, she remained intensely loyal to her husband. The burden of responsibility was too much, however, for him to carry unaided; he became very depressed, and obsessed with the thought that he was a failure. This feeling was intensified when he met Israel again. They had not seen each other for six years, but Israel's attitude was cold and withdrawn, and after a few impersonal words he turned his back on Nicky and walked away. Nicky was deeply distressed, he blamed himself for what had happened to Israel. Gloria tried to encourage him, but in vain. In August 1964 he resigned. He had been at Teen Challenge for two years and nine months.

They left New York and went to live in a small apartment in Houston. Nicky refused the many invitations he received to speak and preach. He felt spiritually cold and found that he did not even want to attend Church any more. With no income, Nicky was at last forced from financial necessity to accept an invitation to preach at a youth crusade. Although he went without any enthusiasm, when he finished his address crowds of young people came to the altar rail to commit their lives to Christ. All at once, Nicky realised that God still had a use for him, even when he was unwilling to be used. With eyes full of tears, he joined those who had come forward, and kneeling down, re-dedicated *himself* to God.

Just before Christmas, he spoke at a meeting of the 'Full Gospel Business Men's Fellowship International'. Through this group of laymen came a flood of speaking engagements which took him, in 1965, to most of America's major cities. A meeting with Dan Malachuk, a New Jersey businessman, led to the re-awakening of his concern for pre-teenage children, known as the 'little people'. Like the older boys and girls, they also wandered the streets, joined gangs and were then involved in fighting and crime, and many of them became addicted to drugs and alcohol. With Dan's encouragement, and with 3,000 dollars contributed at the conclusion of a four-day crusade in Seattle, Nicky and Gloria returned to California and opened an 'Outreach for Youth' Centre in Fresno. A Board of Directors was formed and Nicky recruited staff to assist in his mission to the 'little people' and their parents.

In the Autumn, Nicky returned to New York for a series of speaking engagements. One evening he returned to his hotel to hear his telephone ringing. To his delight he heard a familiar voice say, 'Nicky, it's me, Israel.' The next evening Israel came to the hotel with his young wife, Rosa. As they talked of their days together in the Mau Maus, Nicky reminded Israel of a night when he had saved his life. 'Tonight,' said Nicky, 'I want to tell you something that will *save your* life.' He told Israel that although he had turned away from God, nonetheless God had not rejected him. Israel's eyes filled with tears. He knelt with Rosa while Nicky prayed for them both. With deep emotion, Israel began to pray: 'Lord, forgive me. Forgive me. Forgive me.' He shuddered and then, as though filled with new strength, cried out, 'Lord, I thank you.'

Since then, Nicky Cruz has become well-known, not only throughout the USA, but also internationally. He and Gloria now have four daughters and live in Raleigh, North Carolina, where they have a new headquarters for their *Outreach for Youth* campaign. Nicky also travels all over the world speaking to young people. The area of his outreach has been extended further through the printed, as well as the spoken, word. He has told the story of his life in a best-selling book, *Run, Baby, Run.* He receives thousands of letters a year and, in 1971, a selection of these letters together with his replies, was published under the title, *The Lonely Now.* Two more books have followed, *Satan on the Loose,* and *The Corrupters,* and another book, *The Magnificent Three,* is soon to be published. His story was also told in David Wilkerson's book, *The Cross and the Switchblade,* subsequently made into a film. Two other documentary-type films have been made about Nicky's experiences; they are *No Need To Hide* and *Satan On The Loose.*

His greatest joy has been to lead to Christ those who were once members of his gang. For example, Tooley and China were two former Mau Maus who were converted at a Billy Graham crusade meeting at which Nicky gave his testimony. Afterwards China said to Nicky, 'You've always been our leader. We followed you to hell when you were president of the Mau Maus. Now tonight we've followed you to heaven—and that's much better.' 'That's right,' Tooley broke in. 'Only *you* ain't our leader anymore. Now we've got a *new* leader—right?' Nicky nodded his head. 'That's right, boys, we *all* have a new leader. His name is Jesus.'

ALL those who were members of the Mau Maus when Nicky was their leader have now been converted.

For Further Reading

'Run, Baby, Run': Nicky Cruz with Jamie Buckingham: Logos International, 1963; Hodder and Stoughton Ltd, 1971

'The Lonely Now': Nicky Cruz with Jamie Buckingham: Logos International, 1971; Hodder and Stoughton Ltd, 1973

'Satan on the Loose': Nicky Cruz: Fleming H. Revell Co., 1973, Oliphants, 1973

'The Corrupters': Nicky Cruz: Fleming H. Revell Co., 1974

'The Magnificent Three': Nicky Cruz (to be published)

'The Cross and the Switchblade': David Wilkerson with John and Elizabeth Sherrill: Fleming H. Revell Co., 1962; Spire Books, 1964

Films

'The Cross and the Switchblade': David Wilkerson's ministry to New York teenage gangs, includes the conversion of Nicky Cruz: Col. 85 mins. Don Summers Evangelistic Association, P.O. Box 10, 12-14, The Boulevard, Weston-Super-Mare, Avon, BS23 1NL

'No Need To Hide': documentary in which Art Linkletter with Nicky, retraces the main events in Nicky's career: Col. 55 mins. Don Summers Evangelistic Association or British Youth For Christ (address below)

'Satan on the Loose': documentary in which Nicky returns to Puerto Rico to recreate his early life in order to warn of the dangers of dabbling in Satan worship and the occult: Col. 30 mins. British Youth For Christ Films and Services, 136 Finch Road, Handsworth, Birmingham B19 1HN

For Further Information

Nicky Cruz Outreach: Box 27706, Raleigh, North Carolina 27611, USA

CHAPTER ELEVEN

The Star Stayer

Cliff Richard

Born 1940

The headline in the *New Musical Express* called him 'The Star Stayer'. It was used to describe Harry Rodger Webb, who is now universally known as Cliff Richard. In a nationwide popularity poll, readers of the paper had, for the ninth time, voted Cliff as the 'Top British Male Singer' of the year. In various other polls he had been voted 'Top World Male Singer', 'Personality of the Year.' 'The Artist Who Is The Greatest Credit to Showbusiness' and, in addition, had twice (once with his backing group The Shadows) received the Ivor Novello Award for Outstanding Services to British Music. He had reached the summit of the world of popular entertainment within a very short space of time and, what was so unusual, once there he had remained at the top.

Cliff was born on 14 October 1940, in Lucknow, India, the eldest of four children and the only son of Rodger and Dorothy Webb. When the British Government granted Home Rule to India in 1948, Rodger Webb, who worked for a catering firm, lost his well-paid job and the family had to return to England; Cliff was then eight years old. The Webbs had exactly £5 between them and, unable to buy or rent a house, they went to live with Cliff's grandmother in Carshalton, Surrey, where the five of them had a single room. Cliff attended the local primary school where he became the butt of some unkind teasing—his complexion was so darkly tanned by the sun that the other children called him 'Red Indian Harry' and 'Nigger'. After eighteen months the family moved to live with another relative in Waltham Cross, Hertfordshire, but the accommodation was no better there. The whole family had to make do with one room, and they were even more overcrowded when, soon after their removal, Cliff's mother gave birth to another baby daughter. Fortunately a neighbour reported the cramped conditions in which they were living and a council housing officer called to see for himself; within two months they were allocated a house of their own on a council estate in Cheshunt. They were still very poor, and Cliff's father made their first furniture out of packing cases bought for a shilling each.

Cliff was sent to the Cheshunt Secondary Modern School where he did well at both lessons and sport. He excelled at athletics and football, playing right back for his school and, later, for the County. It was at Cheshunt that he became seriously interested in music. In his younger days he had enjoyed playing records on a portable wind-up gramophone; unfortunately, this had been left behind in India. When Cliff was just fourteen, his father won some money on the football pools and Cliff (with his mother's support) persuaded Mr Webb to buy a record player in preference to a television set. Cliff began to collect records, particularly of Elvis Presley and Bill Haley, both American rock-and-roll singers. He idolised Elvis Presley and spent hours listening to his records, mouthing his words, copying his intonations and imitating his body movements. At school Cliff formed a harmony group which sang un-accompanied at school dances and at the local youth club. When Bill Haley and his Comets came to London, Cliff and some friends went to one of their concerts—though the only way they could obtain tickets was by playing truant from school to join the queue at the box-office. The next day they were punished by the headmaster, who deprived them of their prefects' badges. However, it was a memorable concert for Cliff. That evening, as the Haley Comets pounded out their own style of Rock 'n Roll, he realised that pop music was the only life for him.

Cliff left school when he was sixteen and took a clerical job at the factory where his father worked. Soon after starting work,

Cliff heard that a local skiffle group was looking for a vocalist. He went for an audition and became a member of the Dick Teague Skiffle Group. Although they only played at parties, wedding receptions and local dances, Cliff felt that he had at least taken the first step towards achieving his ambition to be a pop-singer. He was told that he would have to play the guitar as well as sing. Fortunately, he was able to get hold of a cheap, second-hand instrument and he spent several weeks giving hour after hour to practice.

Being in a semi-professional group was exciting for a time, but Cliff and the group's drummer soon wearied of skiffle music and decided to form their own rock 'n roll group. They teamed up with another boy who played the guitar and they called themselves 'The Drifters'. They played in pubs and at dances and even at the 21's Expresso Bar in Soho. They strengthened their group by recruiting a lead guitarist and, equally important, they acquired a manager, John Foster. Their new manager felt dissatisfied with the way they billed themselves as 'Harry Webb and The Drifters', and after some discussion, suggested instead, '*Cliff Richard* and the Drifters'. 'Don't you mean Richards?' someone asked. 'No, I mean Richard, without the "s" ', John Foster replied. 'Everyone will call him Cliff Richards and then we can correct them—that way they'll never forget his name.' They made their first public appearance under their new name at a ballroom in Derby in 1958. From that time on his first name was Cliff and his surname Richard. Even his own family soon forgot that he had been christened Harry Webb. John Foster persuaded an agent, George Ganjou, to hear Cliff and his backing group. The agent was only mildly interested but he recorded them on a demonstration disc which he then sent to Norrie Paramor, a recording manager working for the EMI record company. Norrie Paramor auditioned the group, was impressed by their potential and arranged for them to make their first-ever record. On one side was a song Norrie Paramor provided, on the other side a rock 'n roll number called 'Move It' by Ian Samwell, one of Cliff's own group, The Drifters. The song had been written on the top-deck of a bus en route for one of their shows. While they were waiting for the record to be released, George Ganjou arranged for Cliff to do a four-week season at Butlin's Holiday Camp, Clacton-on-Sea. Cliff insisted that he would appear only if the other members of his group were also booked, and eventually the management agreed. Up to this point, Cliff had done his singing in his spare time. Now he handed in his notice at the factory, and on 9 August 1958, signed a long-term contract with his agent and so became a professional singer.

Towards the end of their month at Butlins, Cliff and The Drifters were thrilled to discover that their record was moving into the popularity charts, their own composition 'Move It' having entered the Top Twenty most popular records; subsequently, it reached the number two position. As a result of the record's success, events began to move with bewildering rapidity. A sensational stage tour of one-night stands, regular television appearances on the ITV pop music show 'Oh Boy!', and a part for Cliff in the film *Serious Charge*, all added up to a dream come true, 'Living Doll', one of the songs in the film, was made into a record by Cliff and The Drifters. It was in the hit parade for six weeks and sold over a million copies, earning one of the coveted 'Golden Disc' awards. The record was not a rock 'n roll number but a 'fairly sophisticated kind of Country and Western ballad'; it was a significant indication that Cliff might outlast the rock 'n roll era and develop into an entertainer of great versatility.

Meanwhile, new and more competent instrumentalists had taken the place of the original members of the group; also there had been two changes of manager. Another alteration was introduced in 1959. To avoid confusion with an American group of the same name, The Drifters changed their name to The Shadows. Later in the year, Cliff took a leading role in the film *Expresso Bongo*; it was in this second film that he made his mark as a cinema personality. His third film, *The Young Ones*, was not only a box-office success but was also widely regarded as the first outstanding screen musical to have been made in Britain. During 1960, Cliff's name appeared in the Top Twenty charts for fifty of the fifty-two weeks. By mid-1961, he had made sixteen records, every one of which had been in the hit parade, twelve of them in the first or second positions, and two of them had sold over a million copies. He had been on the BBC radio show 'Top of the Pops' and had done a six-month season in the show 'Stars in Your Eyes' at the London Palladium. At twenty-one he was already acknowledged as one of the most popular stars in the world of light entertainment. He had achieved his success by hard work and single-minded determination: 'For three or four years', he says, 'we ate, drank and slept pop. We knew to get to the top you had to be dedicated, committed. We were going to the top. . . .'[1] It is greatly to his credit that, when fame and fortune came, Cliff remained unspoilt and natural, earning a reputation as the 'modest star'.

During 1961 an event took place which, at first, cast a dark cloud over Cliff's life, but later proved to be a major turning point in his personal life. His father had been ill for more than a year, and had been taken to hospital in a serious condition while Cliff was abroad on a concert tour. He died shortly after Cliff's return home. Cliff had always enjoyed a secure and happy relationship with his parents, but during his father's twelve months of illness, father and son had grown particularly close to each other. Cliff now felt as though suddenly, life had turned sour. He recalls how, 'night after night I would come home from the studio and sit in Dad's old chair and wonder what the trouble was'.[2] Sometimes, as he sat pondering, his thoughts turned to religion. When he was quite young his parents had taught him to pray each night and while in India he was in a church choir. For some time after their return to England, he and his mother had gone regularly to church. His father was not a church-goer, in spite of the fact that he believed in prayer and often read to the family from the Bible. Cliff, however, had given little attention to religion since the age of fifteen. But now he began to wonder if it might contain something that would meet the sense of emptiness that had followed his father's death.

There followed a tour of Australia with The Shadows, and all the time there was one question uppermost in Cliff's mind: 'If a good man can go the way my father did, then what's life all about? I wanted somehow to reach my father and find out from him what it was like after death, what was going to happen to me.'[3] Cliff decided to go to a spiritualist seance, but Brian Locking (currently The Shadow's bass guitarist) advised him against it. Producing a Bible, he showed Cliff a number of passages which gave warning of the dangers of consulting mediums. Cliff was much impressed. Looking back he says,

> 'It was the very first time in my life that I saw the Bible as having something to say about my problems, about right now. I was surprised at how *hopeful* that thought was. Could it be that behind my wish to contact Dad, I'd really been looking for another Father all the time? A Father who was really there, who could really speak....'[4]

As a result of this conversation with Brian Locking, Cliff abandoned the idea of dabbling in spiritualism.

During the period 1962-63, Cliff and The Shadows were kept very busy. There were overseas tours, a long series at the London Palladium, a summer show at Blackpool, a television series, and the making of a succession of records. In spite of the hectic pace of life Cliff managed to find time to pursue his re-awakened interest in religion. Brian Locking was a devoted Jehovah's Witness and Cliff began to attend their meetings regularly. 'It suddenly hit me', Cliff says, 'that there was more to life than I thought there was—that the things I had weren't satisfying.' Although Cliff came under the influence of the Witnesses for over two years, he held back from becoming a baptised member of the sect. During the time he was reading through the Bible, questioning and discussing. A chance conversation marked a further landmark in his spiritual quest. He often went back to Cheshunt to visit his former English teacher, Joy Norris, a Roman Catholic. On one occasion they discussed religion; Mrs Norris could see that Cliff was not fully convinced by the reasoning of the Witnesses and she arranged a meeting for him with some of her Christian friends. Their sincerity and conviction impressed him. He was invited to join in some of the activities of a local branch of The Crusaders, a Christian youth organisation which meets in groups for Bible study and discussion. He watched and listened; slowly the Christian Faith became more and more meaningful to him. Although he valued the genuine friendship of the Christians he met, it was some time before he would go to church with them. Cliff questioned all that he heard and compared it with what he was reading in the Bible. 'Somewhere in the pages of the Bible', he says, 'I found what I'd been searching for. I found Him. He was the missing element in my life, the element I had been searching for all along. . . .'[5] The searching of Scripture and the eager debate with humanists, Jehovah's Witnesses and people of various religious persuasions brought matters to a head in the Autumn of 1965. Cliff recalls how it happened:

'It all culminated when I suddenly realised that there were certain facts about Jesus that I couldn't dispute. I found that I was believing great chunks about Him. I realised that the most essential things about Him were His divinity and resurrection. I remember reading a scripture which says, "Behold, I stand at the door and knock, and whoever opens the door I will come in." ' [6]

All that was needed now was for Cliff to take that decisive step, and open the door.

One night, after a lengthy discussion with some Christian friends, Cliff asked, 'If I want to be a real Christian exactly what do I have to do?' 'Admit and confess your sin,' he was told, 'Believe that Jesus Christ died so that you could be forgiven, and put your whole trust in Him.'[7] As the gathering broke up Cliff told his host, 'I'm on my way in.'

Looking back at that critical evening, Cliff says, 'It suddenly came to me that really I hadn't opened any doors. Jesus was a reality. He was there, but He hadn't had anything to do with my life.'[8] That night Cliff 'opened the door'. He describes the inward change he experienced as a consequence,

'The dissatisfaction I was going through was eradicated almost immediately. I can't say it went overnight, but there was an emotional feeling when I committed myself to my beliefs. There was a certain amount of relief and, over a period of time, the dissatisfaction went away.' [9]

As a result of his committal to Christ, Cliff became much more 'involved with people' at a deeper level. He says, 'I was always a humanist, I cared in a way about people, but now it's far deeper in that I care for them not only physically but spiritually as well, so that I want to be involved with every aspect of their lives.' [10] In particular, Cliff became much more actively involved with the Crusaders, and in December 1965, he was appointed an assistant leader of the group which met at Finchley. Whenever he could, he shared in their outings, including an Easter holiday on the Norfolk Broads. In subsequent years he took some of the boys for a week's holiday on his own motor launch *Pomander*. Although he was very impressed with The Crusaders, at first attending church meant nothing to him. Then, suddenly, he realised the importance of worshipping in church and meeting regularly with other mature Christians. He joined an adult confirmation class at the Anglican Church of St Paul's, Finchley, and, after some months of instruction, was confirmed by the Bishop of Willesden on 6 December 1966. Today he is more than ever convinced that 'going to Church is vital', not least for 'an artist who is constanly giving something of himself'.

Cliff's spiritual quest had begun when his father died in 1962. Now, four years later, he was a fully committed Christian and a member of the church. During the years of his spiritual search, his reputation as an international entertainment artiste had continued to grow. His concerts were given a tremendous reception all over the world, including countries behind the 'Iron Curtain'. The film, *The Young Ones*, made Cliff a top box-office draw in Britain during 1963, although it was his next film *Summer Holiday* which really established his reputation as a film star. His other musical-comedy films, *Wonderful Life*,

Finders Keepers and *Take Me High* were equally attractive to the cinema-going public. Aware of the need for diversification, Cliff went on stage with The Shadows in the pantomine *Aladdin*, and later in *Cinderella*, both at the London Palladium. In his desire to be a complete all-round performer, Cliff felt the challenge of the theatre and in May 1970 he made his début as a stage actor in the Bromley New Theatre's production of *Five Finger Exercise*. The following year he played in Graham Greene's *The Potting Shed* which subsequently came to the Sadlers Wells Theatre, in London, and which Cliff regards as 'probably the most fulfilling thing I have ever done'. Cliff has twice represented Britain in the Eurovision Song Contest, taking the song 'Congratulations' to second place in 1968, and in 1973 singing 'Power to All Our Friends' which came third.

After he became a fully committed Christian, Cliff was less anxious about his career and professional reputation. In consequence he became more and more relaxed on stage and his audiences were conscious of this and the genuine joy that came across in his performances. He made no secret of his new-found faith and talked quite openly about his convictions to his immediate colleagues and show-business friends. However, to avoid the wrong kind of publicity, he tried to take part in church activities as anonymously as possible. On one occasion, at Christmas, he went to his local hospital to play the guitar and sing. In one of the wards an elderly patient was heard to remark, 'that young man was quite good, really—he ought to take it up as a career!'

In fact, Cliff considered *giving up* show-business, in order to become a full time teacher of religion in school. With this in view, he took and passed the 'O' level examination in Religious Knowledge. However, he came to the conclusion that he could do more good, and exert more Christian influence, by *remaining in* the world of entertainment. Cliff's initial appearances at large public religious meetings took place at the Central Hall, Westminster; first, when he sang at a Crusader rally and later, in April 1966, when he was interviewed before a capacity audience at an Anglican youth rally. The general public, however, did not become aware of Cliff's open profession of Christianity until June 1966, when he sang and spoke at Earls Court during the Billy Graham's Greater London Crusade. The morning after his appearance, every newspaper carried the story. 'It took me quite a long time', Cliff told reporters, 'to pluck up enough courage to tell the world "I'm a Christian" . . . I feel it is my duty and the duty of all Christians, to tell as many people as possible about this wonderful thing I have discovered.' [11]

Cliff began to receive a constant flow of invitations to speak at meetings and religious rallies. He also took part in religious discussion on television. He says, 'It was then I realised that this was the medium I could be most active in, and I have really used it. I don't make any bones about it. I have used my career. I know that this is my way to be an active Christian.'[12] All this was very demanding and he began to feel the need for a deeper knowledge of the Bible and Christian doctrine. During the summer of 1972, he took a break from work and spent some weeks studying at Oak Hill Theological College in North London. As a result he felt much better equipped as an advocate of the Christian Faith.

Cliff has had to face a certain amount of criticism over his decision to remain in show-business. He says

'I find it so frustrating to find people so blind. Can't people believe the Holy Spirit works in many ways? When I'm there on stage or in cabaret I say, I am a Christian and I'm going to sing "When I survey the Wondrous Cross". I also sing some gospel numbers and people listen and some for the first time hear about the Cross.' [13]

Cliff often receives letters from those who have become interested in the Christian Faith through hearing him sing gospel songs at ordinary concert appearances.

In addition to this kind of witness, Cliff has toured Europe as part of the Eurovangelism programme, *Help, Hope, Hallelujah,* and has taken part in Gospel Concerts in Norway, Sweden, Holland, Germany, and Yugoslavia, as well as in most major cities in Britain. He has also acted in two films made by the Billy Graham Organisation. The first was *Two a Penny*, shot in 1967 on location in London, and the second was a documentary on Biblical Israel, entitled *His Land*. In the summer of 1973, Cliff took part in Spre-e '73, a week-long 'crusade' organised by the British Billy Graham Evangelistic Association. It was held at London's Wembley Stadium and several pop music stars took part in an effort to attract young people.

Cliff has had two books published, *The Way I See It,* 1968, (revised edition *The Way I See It Now*, 1973) and *Questions,* 1970. He has also made two albums of religious recordings. By the end of 1973 he was writing more of his own songs and many of these, including a number of gospel songs, are on his album *Help It Along*, released in 1974.

Cliff has a real concern about social questions—often reflected in the songs he chooses for his concerts. He has strong views on the need to uphold moral standards and was the youngest member of Lord Longford's Commission on Pornography. He has also given his support to the Nationwide Festival of Light, appearing at various Festival activities.

He has been actively involved in two other ventures of Christian concern and out-reach. One is The Evangelical Alliance Relief Fund (TEAR), a relief agency which channels its resources through Christian doctors, nurses, agriculturalists and others, working in many different countries. Although it provides emergency aid in areas stricken by earthquake, flood or famine, TEAR's main purpose is to promote self-help, development projects in those lands which make up the 'Third World'. Through the Fund, Cliff has taken a great interest in the problems of Bangladesh, visiting the Bihari Refugee Camps and the Sher-E-Bangla Hospital, Dacca, where some of the medical workers are financed by TEAR. On his return from Bangladesh in November 1973 he said,

'I saw terrible scenes of poverty and since then I've been even more concerned with the use of money. I now make a special point of tithing my time and, in fact, have been cutting down on general appearances, and singing many concerts for TEAR Fund with which I am closely associated.' [14]

The other enterprise in which Cliff has a special interest is The Arts Centre Group (ACG) which he helped to establish. The ACG brings together people who are concerned that Christians should be involved in the Arts—in music, painting, journalism, literature, architecture, drama, films, television and radio. It seeks to encourage young Christians to develop their artistic talents, if possible to the highest professional standard. Hundreds of established artists and students have come together to teach, learn and experiment. At the London Centre in Kensington, there are regular evening meetings and discussions. The ACG also organises weekend conferences and holds public concerts and exhibitions, including an annual Festival of Arts. Cliff is on the organising committee and, as time permits, gives his active help and support to the Centre.

Although Cliff gives a good deal of his time to Christian work, he remains a dedicated professional entertainer. His recordings continue to be best-sellers, his television shows bring him into thousands of homes, his tours are still sell-outs. If asked, he says he does not know what the future holds for him. 'But', he says,

'I believe the Bible means what it says: "All things work together for good for those who love God." I'm prepared to accept that and live my life by it. . . . For me, life is for finding and knowing God. That is why Jesus Christ came into the world, and that is the whole object of our existence on earth.' [15]

If pressed to say what, given the choice, he would like to be in ten years time, his answer is unequivocal, 'I'd like to be a better Christian.' [16]

References

Grateful acknowledgement is made to the Authors and Publishers of the literature cited below. See Further Reading for key to abbreviations.

1. NSNS, p. 158.
2. GP '74, p. 5
3. GP '72, p. 6.
4. GP '74, p. 7.
5. GP '74, p. 7.
6. MS,   p. 18.
7. NSNS, p. 169.
8. MS, p. 18.
9. MS,   p. 18.
10. MS, p. 19
11. NSNS, p. 153.
12. MS,   p. 19.
13. MR.   14. MR.
15. Q, p. 95.
16. GP '72, p. 7.

For Further Reading

'New Singer, New Song': David Winter: Hodder & Stoughton Ltd, 1967 (NSNS 1969)

'My Story': Cliff Richard: World Record Club—free booklet with boxed set of records (MS)

'Questions': Cliff Richard: Hodder & Stoughton Ltd, 1970 (Q)

'The Way I See It Now': Cliff Richard: Hodder & Stoughton Ltd, 1968; revised edition 1973

'Guideposts Magazine'—Brit. Ed. Oct/Nov. 1972: Article by Virginia Kelly. (GP '72)

'Guideposts Magazine'—Brit. Ed. Oct/Nov. 1974: Article by John and Elizabeth Sherrill. (GP '74)

Cliff Richard Talks to Tony Jasper: 'Methodist Recorder', 19 Dec. 1974: Article by Tony Jasper (MR)

'Jesus in a Pop Culture': Tony Jasper: Fontana Books, 1975

Films

Apart from several commercial films in which Cliff Richard has starred, there are a number of films which illustrate his activities as a Christian:

'Life With Johnny': Parables presented by Cliff in a modern musical setting: Tyne-Tees TV 1969. B/W. 20 mins. each

'Johnny Up The Creek' (The Good Samaritan)
'Johnny Faces Facts' (The Mote and the Beam)
'Johnny Come Home' (The Prodigal Son)

'Let's Join Together': features Cliff and other stars during the Billy Graham campaign at Earls Court, Spre-e '73: Col. 60 mins.

'Two A Penny': fictional story starring Cliff as a young lay-about who is influenced by his girl-friend to 'give God a try'. Col. 96 mins.

The above films may be hired from:
World Wide Films, Shirley House, 27 Camden Road, London NW1 9LN

'A Day With Cliff Richard': depicts a typical day showing the more intimate aspects of Cliff's life and illustrating his commitment as a Christian: 1975. Col. 30 mins. On hire from Concordia Films, Viking Way, Bar Hill Village, Cambridge, CB3 8EL; or the Don Summers Evangelistic Association, P.O. Box 10, 12-14, the Boulevard, Weston-Super-Mare, Avon BS23 1NL

'Why Should the Devil Have All the Good Music?' Cliff Richard, Barry Norman and other singers at the London Festival for Jesus: Col. 50 mins. British Youth For Christ Films and Services, 136 Finch Road, Handsworth, Birmingham B19 1HN

Records

Very numerous! A boxed set is available with the Booklet 'My Story' from World Record Club, P.O. Box 11, Richmond, Surrey, TW9 1QP

For Further Information

The International Cliff Richard Movement: P.O. Box 4164, Amsterdam 1005, Holland

The Christian Activities Organiser: 1 Bridgeman Road, Teddington, Middlesex TW11 9AJ

The Arts Centre Group: 19 Draycott Place, London SW3 2BR

Tear Fund: 1 Bridgeman Road, Teddington, Middlesex TW11 9AJ

CHAPTER TWELVE

Friend of the Down-and-Outs

Sally Trench

Born 1947

It was late at night. A sixteen-year-old girl was on her way home after spending a weekend in the country. Crossing London's Waterloo Station she bumped into an old woman dressed in ragged 'cast-offs'. Mumbling an apology she hurried on, noticing a number of dirty, unshaven men trying to sleep on the hard benches along the platform. It would have been all too easy to 'pass by on the other side'; checking the impulse, she turned back, sat down between two of the scruffiest men and gave each of them a cigarette. A large West Indian ambled over, grinned and said, 'You're too pretty to be among us dirty drunks. You're not one of us. Go home.'

Sally Trench took his advice. That night, as she lay in bed, she thanked God for her comfortable home and the love of family and friends. As a child she had been precocious, high spirited and unorthodox. The convent school she had attended could not contain her and, at fifteen, she was expelled. This was one of the turning points in her life, for had she stayed at school and gone on to University, it is unlikely that she would have taken up the work to which she has since devoted her life. In the two years following her expulsion she had done a variety of jobs without finding any that fully absorbed her energy. Now, as she reviewed her life, Sally decided that it was time she did something to help those less fortunate than herself.

The next night, just after midnight, she put a vacuum flask of coffee, sandwiches and cigarettes into a haversack and prepared to leave the house. To avoid waking her father, who was a light sleeper, she climbed out of her bedroom window and descended by a drainpipe. She cycled to Waterloo Station and there found the same destitute men, huddled under old newspapers. She handed them coffee and cigarettes and then cycled home, regaining her room by means of the drainpipe. This was the beginning of Sally's nightly visits to the station. She learned to sleep until 2 a.m., when she would dress and set off on her bicycle, returning home about 4 a.m., without any of her family knowing.

After some months, Sally began to realise that her nightly coffee trips only brought temporary relief. She knew that the dossers needed more permanent care than she or the Welfare State seemed able to provide. One evening, she was walking through one of the poorer parts of London when she came across a down-and-out lying in the gutter, no-one taking any notice of him. She helped him back to where he lived, which turned out to be the Golborne Centre. This was a church in the Portobello Road, no longer used for worship, but now providing shelter for approximately fifty vagrants, delinquents, ex-convicts and inadequates. The Centre was run by a Nonconformist Minister, the Revd 'Bram' (Bertram) Peake.

Sally began to visit Golborne two or three times a week to help wash up or just to talk to the men and young boys who lived there. It was slow work winning their confidence. Bob, an ex-prisoner, was one of those with whom she did succeed. With her help, he obtained work at a bakery and later, Sally was able to re-unite him with his parents. There were many set-backs, even with Bob, but after visiting the Centre for a full year, Sally felt that she had proved the value of sympathy, understanding and genuine concern in helping young delinquents to re-adjust to life.

Through Bram Peake, Sally was introduced to The Simon Community Trust. Named after Simon of Cyrene, who carried the cross for Jesus, the Trust was founded in 1963 by Anton W. Clifford. Anton was a former probation officer, who believed that condemning men and women to homelessness, prison or mental hospitals was no answer to the problems of the individuals concerned or of society as a whole. So he and his trustees founded a series of homes run by the destitute men themselves. The Simon houses became a kind of pipe-line through which dossers, convicts and drug addicts moved from reception centres to Simonwell, a farm in Kent, from which they might return to normal everyday life.

Sally was unable to help with the Simon project for three months owing to a serious back-injury, but when she recovered she gave up her regular secretarial job in order to work full-time with the Simon Community as Anton's personal assistant and, eventually, she became his co-director. Much of their work was done at Simonlight, a derelict house in Stepney, London. Open to everyone, it was dirty but warm, and at weekends, accommodated up to a hundred vagrants, many of whom were addicted to drinking methylated spirits.

One such addict became Sally's special care. Each night, for four months, she went out looking for him on the bomb-sites and brought him back to Simonlight. Like most crude spirit drinkers, his stomach was burned dry and he could not digest solid food. Consequently, before leaving him to sleep, Sally would feed him 'Complan' from a teaspoon. Each morning, after taking some soup, he shuffled off to find more drink; there was never a word of thanks. He became very ill; for two days Sally sat holding his hand, feeding him, bathing his sweating body, and praying that he would come to realise that someone cared about him. A few days before he died, he smiled at her and said, 'Girl, yer the first person who's loved me.' Although Sally wept, she now knew for certain that her unorthodox work was worth while.

For two years, Anton and Sally worked themselves to the point of exhaustion and illness; but there was not enough money coming in and, although it was bitterly disappointing to them, four of the Simon homes had to be closed. Sally left Simonlight in deep distress and walked the streets until she collapsed. She was taken to a mental hospital suffering from nervous exhaustion.

After a week there, she discharged herself and took the decision to spend all her time with the down-and-outs on the bomb-sites of London's East End. She found that the meths drinkers came from very varied backgrounds, some were well-educated men who had been in good jobs, others had come from a poor environment. Sally wanted to discover how they came to be in such a pitiable condition. One of them gave her the clue: he told her that if she was looking for prevention rather than cure, then she should begin with the teenagers. He suggested that she should adopt the clothes and life-style of the beatniks and go to live among them in order to get to know them.

So Sally began to spend some of her time in and around Trafalgar Square, in the West End of London. There she found many young people living rough, most of them addicted to drugs and drink. She began to frequent the cafes where they drifted during the day, hoping to make contact with them. For over two months she was treated with hostility, the beatniks suspecting that she might be a social worker or an evangelist.

At last the breakthrough came, and she was accepted as one of them. She became painfully aware of the far-reaching effects of drugs. Going one night to visit Trix, a young woman heroin addict, Sally found her holding a piece of glass with which she had just slashed her wrist. Sally tried to take the glass from her and a violent struggle took place. Trix broke free and tried to run away. Sally managed to snatch the glass from her, but Trix picked up a brick and crashed in down on Sally's head. When she regained consciousness, Sally found herself in hospital. After she was discharged, she went back to see Trix. She was in the act of injecting heroin into her arm. Neither said anything about the suicide attempt and the fight, but before Sally left, Trix said casually, 'Sorry abaht that do the other night.' The subject was never mentioned again.

Sally now devoted her days to mixing with the beatniks and her nights to visiting the dossers and spirit drinkers. During the day she begged money from visitors to London and with it bought bread, cheese and cigarettes which she deposited in the left luggage department at Charing Cross Station. Later she collected them and made sandwiches in the station waiting room and then went to a stall on the Embankment where she filled her vacuum flasks with tea. About midnight she began her round: starting at Waterloo Station, and finishing around 5 a.m. on the bomb sites of Stepney. The dossers to whom she gave food and drink were a pitiable sight. Dirty and unshaven, with lice on their bodies, some were to be found in the open, huddling together for warmth; others lived in 'derries' (derelict houses), sleeping among rat-infested filth and rubbish. Sally not only brought them food, but also cleaned and dressed their wounds. Some had been injured fighting or from falling on to an open fire when drunk. There were those she was able to take to hospital for treatment; sometimes all she could do would be to sit with one of them as his life ebbed away.

Although rejected by society, the dossers were, in their own way, kind and warm-hearted people, who looked upon Sally as their very special friend. Her work among them was indeed rewarding, but with the beatniks it became more and more frustrating. Sally had become identified with them but she felt that she was doing nothing practical to help them. She was regarded with respect as an intellectual 'beat' (beatnik) and eventually became known as 'Sally the Christian'. Although the beats were not prepared to follow her example, they admired her for the sincerity of her beliefs. One of them, known as Doc, said, 'You're not one of those people that stand up on a soapbox saying what it's like to have Christ in you and how easy it is to be saved. . . .' Scouse, another beat, interrupted crossly, 'I don't believe in all this religion.' Sally replied,

> 'Dear Scouse, this is nothing to do with religion. This is to do with believing in Christ and following His trail from Bethlehem to Calvary on the way He lived and loved. It doesn't mean going to church, taking the sacraments, going to prayer meetings. It's far more simple than that, and a hundred times more difficult—being a Christian is simply being Christ-like.' [1]

Before Christmas, Sally worked in the Post Office to earn

enough money to buy food and cigarettes for the dossers. Some of the beatniks were very impressed at this and promised to help her to distribute them. To Sally's great disappointment, they failed to keep their promise. However, using a van borrowed from her mother, Sally spent Christmas Day collecting food that had been offered from various sources as far afield as Bournemouth and Petersfield. That evening she went to Waterloo Station and, with the help of friends, began the distribution. Then she drove round the derries and open-places, picking up the lonely down-and-outs, bringing them to a central bomb-site where a huge fire was blazing. Sausage rolls, mince pies and mugs of tea were handed out. One of Sally's friends played carols on a trumpet and everyone began to sing. Bleak, despairing, unsmiling eyes were filled with warmth and light. There was laughter and a sense of togetherness—until, at about three in the morning, it was all over and the dossers returned to the squalor from whence they had come.

The Christmas celebration was a highlight in Sally's ministry to the dossers. Inevitably, however, the long hours, the rough life, and going without proper sleep had an adverse effect on her health. She became increasingly aware of a pain in her chest and developed a racking cough. She struggled on with her self-appointed mission until one day she collapsed in the street. She asked to be taken to the home of Vic Ramsay, an evangelist in charge of the Orange Street Mission in Soho, and there she had to have a month of complete rest. While she was recuperating, Vic helped her to see the difference between working for God and working *with* God. Sally came away convinced that her failures were not because of her own weakness but because she had not been drawing on God's strength. She resolved to entrust her life and work to God's direction. It was not long before her renewed faith was put to the test. She was arrested on suspicion of carrying drugs. At the police station she was searched and put in a cell while her story was verified. Panic seized her, the bare walls of the cell seemed to close in on her. She fell to her knees and prayed, 'God, let me out of here.' After a while a policewoman brought her tea and biscuits.

Her inward distress began to subside as some words of Scripture flashed into her mind, 'Without me you can do nothing', and 'I can do all things in him who strengthens me.' When they were satisfied that Sally was not involved in drug-taking, the police allowed her to go. She walked out into the fresh air. In some way she felt changed, her self-reliance was shattered but she had discovered a new trust in God.

She spent the night on the bomb-site. Among a group of dossers she found one of them, Singer, lying unconscious. When Sally had first met him, Singer was hopelessly addicted to jake (a mixture of lemonade and meths). Through her persistent friendship he had eventually given up drinking and had gone to help in the Simon office. After some weeks there, he had slipped back into his old habits and, in a drunken stupor, fell into a bonfire and burnt his leg so badly that it had to be amputated. In spite of his relapse, Sally visited him regularly in hospital and continued to befriend him after he was discharged. It was clear that he now needed urgent re-admittance. Sally knew that he would not be accepted in his present condition, so she hid him in a derry while she mustered some friends who helped her to wash, shave and dress him in clean clothes before taking him back to the hospital. Sally managed to persuade Betty, Singer's 'girl-friend', to go into the same hospital in order that they might both be helped to give up drink. Every afternoon Sally visited the hospital and spent an hour with them. Within a month, however, Betty managed to smuggle in a bottle of spirits to share with Singer. Having consumed it between them, they fled from the hospital and returned to their familiar haunts on the bomb-sites. Once again, Sally experienced a sense of failure.

With five of her meths drinkers in prison, Sally did not visit the bomb-sites so often, but began to spend more of her nights in Soho with the beatniks, sometimes sleeping in a derelict house, sometimes just wandering around the streets and clubs. Often Sally came across some young girl who had come up to London to get away from home, hoping to find freedom and independence. Sally knew the danger they were in, how often they were forced into prostitution and became 'hooked' on drugs. Some she was in time to save, often taking them back to their own parents. Some were less fortunate, like Jinnie, a girl whom Sally found bleeding profusely after attempting a self-induced abortion. In six months Sally had to deal with seven cases of abortion. Jinnie survived, others did not; and those who did often wished they had not. Sometimes boys as well as girls were at risk. Jess, for instance, had once been a well-mannered, intelligent public schoolboy. After three months among the beatniks, he had completely changed for the worse, using the same coarse language and adopting the same aimless way of life as the others who hung around Trafalgar Square. There was also Tony, an alcoholic, but he was at least willing to try to break free. With those like him, who were prepared to try, Sally spent hours 'drying them out' and nursing them back to health. A few recovered completely and were able to work for their living. But all too often, they soon returned to drinking—as Tony did. It was then that Sally felt powerless to help and could only pray that *God* 'would keep his guiding hand on them'. Now and again, she found an opportunity to talk about her own simple philosophy of life: 'Everybody has a right to be loved . . . the meaning of the word love to me is to give. When you stop giving you stop loving. When you stop loving you stop growing.'[2] She, at least, went on loving and giving.

Once again, Sally awoke in hospital. It was ironic that, having survived the danger of living among vagrants, alcoholics and drug addicts, she should be struck down with an allergic reaction to penicillin, prescribed for blood poisoning in the jaw. Like everything that had happened to her, Sally believed that the enforced rest was not without a purpose. She had time to think, 'To review the past and plan out the future'. She tried to trace the guidance of God in the events of the past few months, including a deep disappointment she had suffered. She had fallen in love and was engaged to be married. It was planned that after the wedding the couple would emigrate to Australia. But a fortnight before the wedding, her fiancé broke off the engagement. Sally was deeply hurt. Her first reaction was to throw herself back with new intensity into the work she had been doing among the dossers and beatniks. But how long, she wondered, could she carry on before she, too, was dragged down to the level of those she was trying to help? Moreover, how much could one individual achieve working alone without the support of other people, or of an organisation which would ensure the continuity of the work? Sally came to the conclusion that God meant her to be part of a community, a community builder, not a 'loner'.

She threw away her dosser clothes and returned home. The next few weeks she spent searching for employment in social welfare work. She looked in vain, for although she had nearly four years of practical experience, she had no professional qualifications. Eventually she was persuaded to work for the 'O' and 'A' Levels she needed to enter a college to be trained for work among young people and adolescents. She studied hard during the day but most nights still contrived to visit the dossers on the bomb sites. She also managed to write a book in which she described her experiences with the dossers and beatniks; the manuscript was mostly typed in the waiting room of Waterloo Station.

One night, she visited a derry where she found six men soaked in meths, all in a deep drunken sleep. She did not disturb them, but being very tired herself, pushed some rubbish aside, and lay down on the floor to rest. Suddenly she was wide awake. The derry was on fire. Kicking the drunken dossers awake, she pushed, heaved and rolled the nearest bodies down the stairs. Outside the blazing building she realised that there were two left inside. Sally grabbed an overcoat, threw it over her head, and charged up the stairs. She managed to hoist the younger of the two dossers on to her shoulders. In spite of her pleas, the older man, Joe, refused to move. There was no time to lose. As she stumbled with her burden down through the smoke and flames, she heard Joe cry out, 'Sal, bury me in my boots will you?' Only later did she learn that he had a broken ankle and could not move without help. He had, in fact, sacrificed his own chance to escape for the sake of his younger companion.

Sally gained admission to Westhill College, Birmingham, but did not complete the two-year course. During her first year, her book *Bury Me In My Boots* was published. She could no longer retain anonymity and the pressure of publicity following the success of the book was too much for her and she fled to New York.

The work of caring she had practised in London among young people she now repeated in Harlem and, later, in the slums of Chicago. In the summer of 1968 an incident occurred which she regards as a turning-point in her career. One hot afternoon, she was sitting with a nine-year-old drug addict, a Negro named Jake. A white clergyman came up to them and, recognising that the boy was on drugs, began to question him:

'Son, do you go to Church?'

'No, man, I don't go to no Church.'

'Son, do you read the Bible?'

'No, man, I don't read no Bible.'

'Son, do you have any kind of religion at all?'

'No, man, I have *no kind* of religion at all.'

'Son, do you know what you are?'

At this, Jake stuck out his puny little chest and said, 'Yes, sir, I'm a black *Christian*.'

To which the clergyman replied, 'No, son, you're just *black*.' Sally was so angry that she would have hit the clergyman in the face, but little Jake put a restraining hand on her arm and said, 'Don't hit him, Sally, even the adequate need understanding.'

Sally says,

'I believe that boy knew more about real Christianity than I did or most of us do. I also believe that God put that little boy there for me. I could not get him out of my mind. Since I was sixteen, I had been trying to cure meths drinkers and junkies, most of whom were too far gone to help. Now I wanted to do something for those young enough for there still to be hope.'

Sally returned to England not knowing exactly what God wanted her to do, but sure that He would show her. In June

1970 she initiated *Project Spark*. With the assistance of the Corporation of Leeds she took over a derelict house which was repaired in order to provide a home for teenage boys who, for various reasons, had nowhere to go. Six boys were taken at a time; they came from local Community Homes (formerly known as Approved Schools) or Borstals; all had a substantial record of delinquency and crime. Through lack of staff the Hostel had to be temporarily closed in 1974, but was reopened the following year as a Family Evening Centre.

The Centre has extended the scope of the work as it caters for up to a hundred 'latch-key children', aged between nine and fifteen years; they come from the immediate neighbourhood, which is one of the poorest in Leeds. The usual recreational facilities are provided such as table tennis, boxing, snooker, dancing and drama, but there is a growing demand for such creative pursuits as woodwork, handicrafts and cookery. Sally hopes that some of the young people themselves will eventually help to run the Centre. She comments on the Project,

> 'Perhaps it is significant that in an area where muggings are commonplace and Saturday night knifings a way of life, there has been no thieving, vandalism or graffiti on the walls of what the kids like to call "our club". We could accommodate double these numbers if we had the facilities and the resources.'

With the Leeds Project established, Sally moved to London. She was loaned a good-sized house by a friend already involved in Project Spark. She moved in and, for the next six months, prayed that God would show her what to do next.

It was not long before Sally noticed a number of children roaming the streets when they should have been at school. She met with the headmaster of the local comprehensive school and discussed the problem with him. After much consideration, the idea evolved of using Sally's house as a home-based unit to give special attention to a small group of children who were unable to cope with full-time education and, consequently, were actual or potential truants. The Inner London Education Authority gave their consent to establishing such a unit for a trial period of six months.

The experiment was a success and the Education Authority agreed to pay Sally as an Education Welfare Officer and to increase the school's staff quota to allow for a part-time teacher to work with Sally. In the summer term of 1974, two groups of children, aged eleven to fifteen, were selected to spend two days a week at Sally's home on condition that they attended the school itself for the other three days of the week.

Sally now has a full-time teacher working with her, but the pattern of teaching adopted at the beginning of the project is basically the pattern still followed. The mornings are spent learning basic subjects, particularly English and Mathematics, with individual tuition based on the child's own needs. In the afternoon there is a choice of practical activities such as art, model making, dress-making, sculpture, weaving and cookery. There is also the opportunity for the usual sports, and other outdoor activities including horse-riding, ice skating and kite flying; in addition there are regular outings to places of interest.

When the children first come they are usually uncooperative and sometimes violent. Sally says,

> 'We have had chairs thrown at us, bricks through the windows, and we've been threatened at knife point. But we are not afraid of confrontation. We believe that discipline is essential because it provides security, and, once you have it, you don't need to enforce it.'

Illiteracy is one of the children's main problems, Sally explains,

> 'These children are ashamed of themselves if they can't read and write and consequently are unable to keep up with those who can. We treat them as adults, not as problem children. Our aim is to build up their confidence until the time when they themselves ask to return to school full time. We also aim to help them to be more sensitive to the needs

of others, which we do through example rather than by preaching.'

Sally has found that the children think of her house as their second home rather than a part of school. The informal home atmosphere is an important aspect of the project. Each week she takes a pair of them, girls or boys, to do the household shopping. She gives them the shopping list and money and lets them learn for themselves how to buy economically.

The children look upon Sally as a mother, friend and confidante. They know that they can go to her at any time with their worries and problems. If there has been a row in their own homes they may suddenly turn up in the evening, or they may just drop in to sit and chat or watch television. Sometimes Sally is called out at night to help find a child who may not have gone home or who has run away from home. Like any mother, she is never completely off duty.

The work Sally is doing now is as demanding as her days and nights spent with the dossers and beatniks. She is still Director of the Leeds Project as well as Project Spark London, and is responsible for raising at least £10,000 a year for the joint enterprise. In all that she has done, both her motivation and sustaining power has been a very strong religious faith.

'The basis of all my work,' she says, 'is my love for Christ, and every human person to me is Christ, however bad they may *seem* to be. In a way, my relationship with God is very similar to that which I have with my children. I love him absolutely, as I love these children. I think of him as a friend with whom I can talk at any time of the day. In fact, he's just the best friend I've ever had, he is everything to me.'

In spite of her deep convictions, Sally gives no impression of religiosity. Probably the most fitting comment on her life was made by one of the Trafalgar Square beatniks who said, 'She's not like the others. . . . Sally won't preach, she's not a religious fanatic—just a *working Christian*.' [3]

References

Grateful acknowledgement is made to the Author and Publisher of:
1. 'Bury Me In My Boots': Sally Trench: Hodder and Stoughton Ltd, Pbk.
    Ed. 1970, p.88   2.   Ibid, p. 167.   3.   Ibid, p. 175.

For Further Reading

'Bury Me In My Boots': Sally Trench: Hodder and Stoughton Ltd, 1968; Pbk.
Ed. 1970

'Down Among the Dead Men'—Faith In Action Series: Brian Peachment:
REP 1974

Films

'Golborne—One Man's Answer': the work of the Revd Bertram Peake at the
Golborne Centre (mentioned in this story). B/W. 30 mins.

On Vagrancy (V), Alcoholism (A) and Drug Addiction (D):

(V) 'No Fixed Abode': BBC (Schools) TV 1973: B/W. 20 mins.

(V) 'No Room at the Doss House': BBC TV 1973: B/W. 50 mins.

(V) 'Christmas Down and Out'—Christmas party for Dossers at Covent Garden:
B/W. 30 mins.

(A & V) 'The Foxes Have Holes': BBC TV 1973: B/W. 30 mins.

(A & V) 'Edna, the Inebriate Woman'—features the work of the Cyrenians and
Christian Action: BBC TV 1971: B/W. 90 mins.

(D) 'Gale Is Dead': BBC TV 1970. B/W. or Col. 50 mins.

(D) 'Monkey on the Back': NFP Canada 1956. B/W. 30 mins.

(D) 'Johnny Go Home'—features the plight of teenagers alone in London:
BBC TV 1975: B/W. 2 parts: 60 mins. each

These films and many others on the same subjects can be hired from: Concord
Films Council, Nacton, Ipswich, Suffolk, IP10 0JZ; a full catalogue can be
purchased.

Filmslides

(D & A) 'Gale in Hospital': 12 slides: Ref. S616: The Slide Centre Ltd, 143
Chatham Road, London SW11 6SR

For Further Information

Project Spark—Director: Sally Trench

    Registered Address: 62 Brook Street, London W1Y 2DB
    London Project: 19 Menelik Road, London NW2 3RJ
    Leeds Project: 90 Shepherds Lane, Chapeltown, Leeds LS8 4LG
The Cyrenians, 13 Wincheap, Canterbury, Kent

The Simon Community Trust, 129 Maldon Road, London NW5

Christian Action, 2 Amen Court, London EC4

Postscript

Mother Teresa on Joy

'We all long for heaven where God is, but we have it in our power to be in heaven with him right now—to be happy with him at this very moment. But being happy with him now means:

> loving as he loves,
> helping as he helps,
> giving as he gives,
> serving as he serves,
> rescuing as he rescues,
> being with him twenty-four hours,
> touching him in his distressing disguise.'

From *Something Beautiful for God*: Malcolm Muggeridge